Finding
Art's
Place

Finding Art's Place

experiments in contemporary
education and culture

NICHOLAS
PALEY

Routledge / New York and London

Published in 1995 by
Routledge
29 West 35 Street
New York, NY 10001

Published in Great Britain in 1995 by
Routledge
11 New Fetter Lane
London EC4P 4EE

Printed in the United States of America.

Library of Congress Cataloging-in-Publication Data
Paley, Nicholas
Finding art's place: experiments in contemporary education and culture / by Nicholas Paley
p.   cm.
Includes bibliographical references and index.
ISBN   0-415-90606-7 (cloth) —   ISBN   0-415-90607-5
(paper.)
1. Arts—Study and teaching (Elementary)—United
States.
2. Minority Students—Education—Arts.   3. Arts and
society—United States.   I. Title
NX304.P35 1995   94-22085
700'.7'073—dc20   CIP

CONTENTS

Acknowledgments

As in many books, the writing here initially looks backward in time. Two decades ago, during my very first week of graduate study at the University of Wisconsin, I had the good occasion to be assigned Michael Apple as a mentor for coursework in curriculum and instruction. It is he who stands in my memory as the first professor who took seriously the status of the artistic as a critical variable in educational thinking and practice. In his classes and seminars, he variously assigned or referenced the writings of Dwayne Huebner, Maxine Greene, Rudolf Arnheim—specifically inviting students to consider the kinds of understandings their work brought to bear on educational study. He privileged the work of practicing artists by discussing them in class. He talked about (and exhibited) Norman McLaren's experimental films. He spoke admiringly of the work of Käthe Kollwitz. Coming almost directly from undergraduate school, where I had studied art and art history, I found such views welcoming. In fact, I found them surprising. In time, I came to recognize how rare these views were, for much of my other coursework that year focused on the empirical and the objective: thinking as straightline, clearline. Perhaps even more to my benefit, though, was how he provided the opportunities (as well as the resources) for students to struggle with articulating how the artistic is a question for the educational through academic projects that invited experimentation with the multiple ways that knowledge might be produced. While a considerable emphasis along these lines was accorded to exploring the languages and inventive possibilities of filmmaking, he was always open to and supportive of other forms of artistic production. That this book appears at all is, in large part, due to this kind of long-standing intellectual encouragement. Michael Apple encouraged his students to take risks, and by so doing, opened spaces for an imagination of difference before such practice became a name.

Other people and institutions helped make this book possible. Special thanks need to be given to Tim Rollins, and Nelson Savinon, Carlos Rivera, Angel Abreu, Victor Llanos, and the late Christopher Hernandez of K.O.S. for their ongoing cooperation in this project. Their studio was always open to visit and they were readily available to discuss their work, often during the most hectic days of last minute preparation to meet exhibition openings or deadlines. They graciously answered any question about their method of artistic/educational practice at any time. Many thanks also to Jim Hubbard, Linda Posell, Marie Moll, and Rachel Clark at The Shooting Back Education and Media Center in Washington, D.C., which was the focus of my inquiry of this multi-sited project; and the children at the New Community Center—in particular, William Cawthorne, Angie Campbell, Tameka Atkinson, Sabrina Greeley, Savon MacLemore, and Michael Sesay, who welcomed me into their photography group with interest and zest; and the volunteers and staff at Shooting Back who provided continuous support for this project. Three original members of the Shooting Back project, Dion Johnson, Charlene Williams, and Daniel Hall, found time to talk about their former and current work when they were busy with many school and community projects. I am indebted to them for their openness and also to their mentor, Ella McCall-Haygan, who also found space in her schedule to discuss their work with me. The staff at the Video Data Bank in Chicago, especially Ayanna Udongo and Mindy Faber, were most helpful in providing the primary visual documentation and background material about the work of Sadie Benning. The paintings of Tim Rollins and K.O.S. that are displayed in this book are courtesy of Mary Boone Gallery; Ron Warren was responsible for extending the loan of their visual documentation to accomodate revised publication schedules. Overall, this project benefited greatly from the support of all these individuals. Without their assistance, this book could not have been produced.

I received much good advice from readers within the academy who commented on various parts of the book as it progressed. It is certainly not their fault that I didn't always act on their thoughtful suggestions. Paul Shumaker read and then outlined crucial revisions on an early version of the theoretical framework for this project, providing models for thinking about initial conceptual organization. Joel Taxel made suggestions that supported the accent on the artistic when I was less than certain of its effectiveness. Janice Jipson read and reread the entire manuscript in its many versions; eventually, I couldn't ignore her repeated recommendations to ("for the hundredth, thousandth, billionth time") follow my inclinations in constructing a book that would experiment with disciplined systems of analytic practice, that would push ideas of artistic representation of educational issues to their limits. Her understandings and insights also served as a reminder that such textual production was not an expression of an oppositional standpoint, but one of difference and independent affirmation. Kari Lokke, who was simultaneously engaged in exploring the politics of writing in her own scholarship, provided long distance clarification and intuitive support. My colleague at George Washington University, Linda Mauro, examined nearly every word of every idea with her intelligent eye; often her suggestions for textual improvement were lengthier than the manuscript in question itself. My students at George Washington University, particularly Honora Mara, Louise Brooks, K. B. Basseches, and Bill Ritter variously read and critiqued selected versions of the chapters on Tim Rollins and K.O.S. and Sadie Benning; their critical observations helped considerably in the shaping of the present versions of these chapters. Maxine Freund, department chair, was supportive of this project throughout; her administrative decisions cleared valuable spaces and time for writing which made it possible for the book to be completed within most editorial deadlines. I am also indebted to George Washington University for granting a sabbatical leave which supported the completion of this book.

Individuals outside the academy contributed much pertinent guidance. Christine Smith provided insights into the workings of bricolage and collage on book pages through personal discussion and by her own artistic practice. Barbara Taff spent many hours working through variations of book graphics/layout/design. Stewart Cauley and Mike Esposito at Routledge saw an intriguing opportunity to experiment with the structure and design of an academic text when an initial mock-up of the project was finally delivered to them, perhaps in a form they had not been anticipating.

Last, many, many thanks to my editor, Jayne Fargnoli, who initially saw promise in this project and then determinedly, skillfully guided it through the multiple stages of its evolution and production. Her patience, editorial suggestions, and expert direction over a three-year period were absolutely instrumental to this project's completion.

Beyond these acknowledgements, or perhaps because of them, I have come to recognize the deeply interconnected nature of authorship. The writing is really many writings. Imagination goes all the way round.

Dedication

All royalties from *Finding Art's Place: Experiments in Contemporary Education and Culture* will go, in equally divided amounts, to the Art and Knowledge Workshop, Sadie Benning, Shooting Back Education and Media Center, and Dion and Friends.

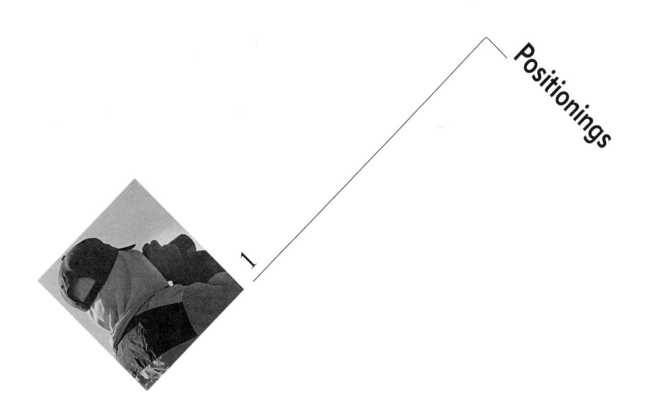

1

Positionings

There have to be disciplines, yes, and a growing acquaintance with the structures of knowledge; but, at once, there have to be the kinds of grounded interpretations possible only for those willing to abandon "already constituted reason," willing to feel and to imagine, to open the windows and go in search.

—Maxine Greene

Reflections from the Heart of Educational Inquiry, 1991

QUESTIONS OF WHETHER CHILDREN AND YOUTH HAVE ANYTHING to contribute to a society's cultural capital are customarily so self-answering that any other view of the issue seems startling. Familiar educational notions have traditionally identified young people as "students" or "pupils," locating them in passive cultural roles where—under varying conditions of supervision—they are expected to serve a kind of apprenticeship, gaining the skills, dispositions, and knowledge that the adults of a given society deem important for them to possess. It is only at some later chronological point, after they have demonstrated a certain level of accomplishment, that youngsters are permitted to engage (albeit differently on the basis of ability, appearance, gender, color, and class) in the various tasks of cultural practice. During their early years, however, those domains of culture associated with the making of discourses, histories, and systems of representation are, for the most part, a closed case. In the economies of cultural production, the years of childhood are only a bridge to a future time.

Such essentialized ideas about the construction of cultural meanings, the agency of children and youth, and the politics of imagination are currently being challenged by a small number of unrelated, non-school projects asymmetrically located across the contemporary social landscape. It is precisely at these sites—situated primarily in what are thought to be the shadowed zones of metropolitan areas—that a number of children and youth, working independently or in collaboration with adults and/or each other, are struggling with the realities of imaginative and cultural production through the varied energies of the arts. On the basis of conventional assessment procedures, many of the young people involved in these projects would be assigned to the lowest groups in their classrooms. Outside the academy, their work provides alternate indices of their capacities.

I came across what may be the longest-lived of these projects unexpectedly in January, 1987, reading a review in *Artforum* about an exhibition in New York of the artistic/cultural/educational work of Tim Rollins (an artist and former South Bronx junior-high-school teacher) and K.O.S., or Kids of Survival (a group of teenagers from that part of the city).[1] From this review, I learned that Rollins and K.O.S. worked together in an after-school project called the Art and Knowledge Workshop, where they collaborated to explore the various connections between literature/art and their daily lives in the South Bronx. A key part of this collaboration was reading classic works of world literature and then transforming them into visual works of art. Using texts as widely divergent as Franz Kafka's *Amerika*, Stephen Crane's *The Red Badge of Courage*, and Lewis Carroll's *Through the Looking Glass* as a starting point, Rollins and K.O.S. would read these books together, discuss their various meanings, then literally tear them apart, using their pages as a base upon which they would then paint a series of images that related the books' meanings to their own lives. I later learned that one of the results of this collaboration was an ongoing series of paintings which were regularly shown in gallery spaces and major exhibitions nationwide.

I recall being immediately attracted to their work. As a teacher educator exploring links between education and the arts in areas beyond those Cameron McCarthy has identified as "the current privileged theoretical and political concerns of the imperial center"[2] (or, first-world, school-based studies), I particularly liked how their project brought forward "peripheral" experiences and voices, articulating them into artworks of unusual impact and power. Even though the review in *Artforum* only hinted at the paintings' visual complexity, I found their presentation deeply compelling, and active with urgent, complex meaning. I was also struck by how Rollins and K.O.S.'s collaboration seemed to forge connections across a plurality of forces not generally addressed by formal pedagogy: impulses related to the political and the poetic, the ideal and the intuitive, the canonic and the contemporary, making and breaking—"learning and burning" (Rollins's expression).

It was during this time that I also became aware of other sites where similar individual and group projects were taking place. Because it is in the city where I work, I learned about Jim Hubbard and his efforts in photography with homeless and "at risk" children in Washington, D.C. at the Shooting Back Education and Media Center. I also heard about "Voices From the Streets," an acting troupe of inner-city children and adults in Washington, D.C. whose performances were linked to a socially active agenda. The staff at Randolph Street Gallery in Chicago told me about the complex, diaristic video productions of Sadie Benning, a high-school dropout from Milwaukee, Wisconsin, who used a Fisher-Price Pixelvision toy video camera to explore her emerging sexual identity and the visual possibilities of self-definition. It was at the Video Data Bank at the School of the Art Institute also in Chicago that I came across the work of Branda Miller (a video artist, curator, and editor), video projects that engage city youth in actively examining issues such as drug use, teenage pregnancy, and school attendance. On a less defined terrain, I also encountered the cultural interruptions and fugitive iconographies of the graffiti artists. Most recently, I heard of Wendy Ewald's work in teaching children from low-income backgrounds to use photography to document their lives, families, and neighborhoods.

Perhaps it was the very peripherality of these projects that made them stand out so insistently. Provisional in terms of life-span, generally unconnected to the disciplined specificities of conventional school knowledge and practice, and located in the shifting interstices of contemporary urban life, their existence placed into abrupt relief many of the mainstream objectives prescribed for children and youth by official educational representatives: notions like performance-based learning, isolated subject mastery, attaining an economic edge, finding a competitive niche, meeting Goals 2000. Measured against the contours of this "high-end" talk were the energies of languages that seemed, educationally speaking, overlooked, ignored, left out.

Artistically, several of these projects had, like Rollins and K.O.S., gained considerable critical attention. The photographs by homeless children in Jim Hubbard's "Shooting Back" were shown in a major exhibition in Washington, D.C., then as a national and international traveling exhibition. Wendy Ewald was a recipient of a MacArthur Award in 1992. And Sadie Benning's videotapes were screened at numerous national and international film festivals, with one of her latest works also selected for the 1993 Biennial Exhibition at the Whitney Museum of American Art.

The more I learned about these forces emerging outside the academy, the more their existence seemed to complicate customary definitions of children's capacity within and across knowledge relations. In time, the complex associations related to several of these projects' forms, textures, and occasions provoked demands in me beyond mere interest. Since little was written about them, at least from an educational perspective, I began to imagine a small collection of writings addressing their individual existence—but also speaking to issues that might be connected in ways perhaps as asymmetrically un/related as the projects themselves. At the time, I speculated that some of these issues might include, but not be limited to, the following: the engagement of children in the construction of social and cultural materials; the kinds of representation that counted in culture and why; the place of art in children's lives; the role of children as artists in society; and the dynamics of what the artist Elizam Escobar has thoughtfully called "the power of the imagination's struggle."[3] It was along these lines that an idea for a book tentatively emerged, one that I began to see could work on differential terrain simultaneously, unevenly—even ambiguously—and one that I felt might connect many of the issues related to art and education, children and imagination, culture and politics in noncompartmentalized ways. It was from these preliminary speculations that, in late 1991, the research and writing for this book began.

———————

From the outset, the more fundamental but perhaps less visible characteristics of this effort involved working through a paradox: How to write about these artistic interruptions without stereotyping thinking about the artistic? By this I mean, how to explore—but simultaneously maintain—the complex nature of these projects' potential range of meanings, associations, and understandings without collapsing their energies into a closed system by consolidating them within any single language, style, or theory?

Since the reality of this question is also central to much debate in contemporary educational criticism (here I refer to the different efforts of a growing number of educators whose work resists analytic structures grounded in unified theoretical systems by targeting the ways such structures repress contradictory articulations and experiences and/or by displacing the idea of a unified analytic with critical strategies that are multiply sited and shifting[4]), I want to key here its importance for this project, emphasizing in the next several pages the theoretical reroutings that were central to the structuring of the writing in this book. The alternative analytic and compositional arrangements to be found here are the result of a conscious decision to construct a textual orientation functioning at a slant to official narratives of educational power.

Beyond the tactical nature of these reroutings, such a move also points to important metacritical issues in educational study: namely, concerns related to the kinds of forms considered legitimate for representing knowledge (why restrict analytic expression to forms of "already constituted reason"?); the character of these forms' terms and propositions (why certain inscriptions and language systems instead of others?); the struggle to bring forward issues of spectatorship and educator identity (why continue the fiction of writer invisibility by repressing the articulation and formulation of subjectivity as a fundamental component of analytic inquiry?); and the process by which one goes about making the mechanics of such deliberations explicit and clear. In what follows, I intend to show how writing about these projects presented an opportunity for working through such issues concretely, but from perspectives that left their naming provisional. It is to an explanation of this opportunity and these interests that I now turn.

The writing in this book is constructed along the lines of several various and variously related modes of address. Broadly speaking, these multiple lines of address explore indirections. They deliberately avoid recognizable discourses of official educational traditions, whose disclosures seem frequently informed by patterns of unified narrative, forms of global thinking, and assumptions of ownership (of history and time, experience and identity, personal value and cultural development). Such totalizing approaches—characterized in a broader critical context as "the classic attempts to see everything steadily and see it whole…[from] a vertical view downward"[5]—have been compellingly challenged across a variety of disciplinary areas by more than a decade of important, sustained work in the different modes of poststructuralist and feminist thinking.[6] Drawing support from and sympathetic to this rich body of work, I saw an opportunity to construct an analysis that would bring forward "diverse, hidden, necessary points of view"[7]—gestures not normally admitted in authoritative educational narratives—by accomodating critical engagements like those Nancy Miller has offered: *"a process of reading through* [a series of multiply positioned intertextualities], *rather than towards* [a sequence of serially arranged arguments leading to a fixed ideological point]…."[8]

More specifically, these intertextualities are constructed through the following modes of address: nonobjective artistic practice, bricolage, polyphonous voice, and the rhizomatic (this order is not hierarchical). Distinct but connected, separate but intersecting, these modes frequently interpenetrate each other's territory, venture across each other's boundaries, and resist analytic compartmentalization. Despite their fugitive tendencies and the dangers and difficulties inherent in specifying or containing them by definition, each of these modes of address is discussed further and separately below.

Nonobjective Artistic Practice

"How is educational study an issue for art?" is a question that, during the past several decades, has been differently taken up with increasing interest by a growing number of educators dissatisfied with positivist ways of talking about educational study and practice.[9] Over the years, one of the most thoughtful of these individuals has been Maxine Greene, who, in many of her writings on education, has explored the power of artistic stances and their relation to educational work. Drawing on her deep engagements with the varied energies of the arts, she has repeatedly argued their importance to pedagogic theorizing and practice, perceiving such approaches as similar to "shifts of attention [which] make it possible to see from different standpoints; they stimulate the 'wide-awakeness' so essential to critical awareness, most particularly when they involve a move to the imaginary—away from the mundane."[10]

More recently, Trinh T. Minh-ha has spoken pointedly to the requirements of explicitly linking these kinds of shifts in critical perspective to a politics of inquiry—especially when addressing modes of artistic practice:

> Every artistic excursion and theoretical venture requires that boundaries be ceaselessly called to ques-

tion, undermined, modified, and reinscribed. By its politics of transformation, critical inquiry is ever compelled to look for different approaches to the aesthetic experience, different ways of relating to it without categorizing it. Different inquiry by its very inquiry; different attitudes of self through knowledge, different knowledge of the self through the selves within (without) oneself. To maintain the indeterminacy of art, criticism is bound to test its limits, to confront over and over again the legitimation of its own discourse, hence to bring about its own indeterminacy.[11]

Connected to these and other[12] voices articulating the imperative to explore artistic modes of analytic representation, the writing in this book is structured as an experiment to open up the sphere of educational study to a logic of expression that "tests limits" much in the ways that the projects discussed here seem to do themselves. In claiming this intensive mode of address, I attempt to more sharply frame the question, "How is educational study an issue for art?" from a perspective that serves *unregulated* forces—("to come up with something that can't be contained, something that both formally punctures [the] existing language on the subject and then, through that hole, pours new information, provocation, and radical juxtapositions to provoke not the sympathy, but the imagination of the viewer[reader])"[13]—rather than reproducing perspectives where art might serve *normalizing* forces that smooth out experience into objectified analytic arrangements.

The idea of developing an inquiry that resisted analytic objectification by merging educational thinking with such an artistic practice was most satisfying when I imagined it at its most open point.[14] It was at such an expressive location, however, that such an address simultaneously generated the greatest pressure—since claiming this kind of stance ran against the grain of suppositions that define disciplined analytic practice: the need to write as "a good academic"; the need "to stay within the lines"; the need to contribute to "narratives of educational tradition." The complex tensions generated by these contradictory requirements (personal and professional, private and public, autonomous and authoritative) created a hybrid of energies that pushed open fissures in conventional frameworks of educational inquiry. "Zone[s] of possibility,"[15] Walker Percy once called these kinds of nonobjective critical opportunities. Why not make use of them? Why not *exploit* them?

Bricolage

Closely related to the address of nonobjective artistic practice is the notion of bricolage. Variously theorized across disciplines during the twentieth century, bricolage has been encoded as an artistic strategy (initially developed by the Dadaists and Surrealists as a method that juxtaposed unrelated, incongruous elements in order to liberate understanding from the mystifications of straight-line thinking); as an anthropological concept (to describe the means whereby "primitive" cultures conceptualize and organize their environments); and recently, as a cultural term (to clarify practices, within certain youth subcultures, of appropriation/juxtaposition serving to disrupt/reorder systems of meaning and discourse).[16] I apply bricolage here in its artistic sense—as an analytic method that reflects its definition as a "term for improvisation...sometimes applied to artistic works in a sense similar to collage: an assemblage improvised from materials ready to hand, or the practice of transforming 'found' materials by incorporating them in a new work." [17]

Several pivotal reasons warrant exploring the potential of bricolage as a language of analytic address.[18] Characterized in large part by visual realities, by discontinuity and juxtaposition in overall form, and by a decentered, porous association among its discontinuous parts, bricolage provides a working alternative to compartmentalized systems of knowledge production/display.

As a visual heuristic, for example, bricolage challenges analytic processes that construct descriptions of reality in exclusively discursive ways, making available a particular kind of strategy for exploring the expressive possibilities of graphic reference as a primary variable in analytic representation. Central to this particularity is the modernist acknowledgement of the multiple, interruptive energies of the visual medium, especially when applied to critical work. Through the address of bricolage, images can be constructed to serve allusive rather than argumentative purposes. They can be produced to problematize rather than decorate statement. Images can be "read" as text. Text can figure as image. Visually, bricolage provides the potential to repoliticize analytic shapes, opening criticality to less partitioned space.

As an inconclusive, discontinuous form, bricolage also creates a sphere for the articulation of "difference" in representation where difference is not objectified as something "other" to be fit within the framework of a more totalized system, but rather, as has been pointed out by writers working in parallel critical contexts, as expressive of a "juxtaposition" of phenomena "on the move, sometimes in synch, more often, in collision." [19] Bricolage affirms these recognitions and helps resist the objectification of multiple experiences into narrative systems which, through patterns of power/knowledge, too often organize difference into hierarchy, or essentialize its energies into a cultural formula inflected by linearity. The tactics of juxtaposition challenge such reductions that collapse heterogeneity and differing motivations into sequence stories and ideology.

Or, from still another standpoint and as an analytic countermethod, bricolage invites a mechanics of interpretation serving imaginative rather than doctrinal concerns. By refiguring the page as an invention, bricolage provides for the possibility of creating an intertext, a no-space and an everyplace where writing can shift from topic to topic—"a sphere whose center is everywhere and periphery nowhere [and which] demands a high level of participation but excludes the idea of goal and direction." [20]

Allusive, shapeshifting, visual: bricolage contributes to an analytic that bears on the kind of criticality that Edward Said identifies as crucial to the development of a "fully articulated program of interference" in the "politics of interpretation." For such a project, the particular accent that bricolage places on the visual is especially enabling since, as Said also notes, "the visual faculty" is a useful medium "to restore the nonsequential energy of lived historical memory and subjectivity as fundamental components of meaning in representation," as well as "to tell other stories than the official sequential or ideological ones produced by institutions of power."[21]

Polyphonous Voice

The writing in this book is also structured along a line of address that reflects a radical shift in thinking about the ways that meanings are made, positioned, and produced in contemporary culture. Central to this important shift are several related recognitions that have been theorized across a complex cultural, pedagogical, and epistemological field. These recognitions include the acknowledgement that the inclusion of multiple voices affirming the multiple realities and experiences of individuals is fundamental to the construction of meaning and to the process of representation; that conventional analytic perspectives, routinely grounded in systems of univocal discourse, fail to effectively reflect the multiplicity of voices essential to the process of meaning-making; that such exclusion creates discursive practices which provide a reductive, artificial view of understanding and human experience; and that the construction of knowledge is a relational activity in which no one particular vocality can assure itself an absolutely authoritative status to the exclusion of others.

The address of polyphonous voice affirms these recognitions, and I further structure it here to provide a presentation of multiple realities and experiences within a framework that reflects a variety of modes of voice. By variously integrating the personal, the poetic, the discursive, and the symbolic, this form of address displays an elasticity, layeredness, and reversibility in vocal status ("the sliding up and down the scales of importance, the destruction of scales of importance"),[22] thereby exploring a range of associations generally excluded (repressed?) from conventional analytic discourse.

While an increasing number of stylistically unconventional approaches to doing critical work related to notions of polyphonous voice have appeared in other disciplinary areas,[23] Patti Lather's insights concerning the importance of developing and implementing this address in educational studies are particularly worthy of note:

> Data might be better conceived as the material for telling a story where the challenge becomes to generate a polyvalent data base that is used to *vivify* [original italics] interpretation as opposed to "support" or "prove." Turning the text into a display and interaction among perspectives and presenting material rich enough to bear re-analysis in different ways bring the reader into the analysis via a dispersive impulse which fragments univocal authority. Such writing works against the tendency to become the locus of authority; it is writing that probes the blind spots of the interpretaters' own conceptualizations and attends to its own constitutive elements.[24]

Lather's idea of "polyvalence" enlisted as a criticality that serves enlivening rather than objectifying determinations suggests an array of non-derivative possibilities for "staging knowledge" (her term). On the one hand, these possibilities challenge conventional analytic systems rooted in teleological discourse (since they provoke the question: "Whose telos?"); on the other, they open up spaces for exploring a transformative educational study and practice where transformation "requires a certain freedom to modify, appropriate, and reappropriate without being trapped in imitation."[25] Such an analytic stance is more than a theoretical conceit or an aesthetic appropriation. Rather, by resisting the objectifications of centralized location, controlled narrative, and systems of closure, such practice acknowledges the radically indeterminate status of experience itself—and, in the case of this writing project, of artistic experience in particular, for, as Trinh T. Minh-ha observes

> [i]f art can be neatly contained in systematic forms of closure, if it can be made to be an object of knowledge, then it no longer is art. Its very "essence" rests upon its elements of inexplicability and of wonder. Or else, why would anyone engage in artistic work, whose value lies precisely in its inability to prove itself worth the price or the attention demanded?[26]

The address of polyphonous voice as structured in this writing project reflects these theoretical recognitions and analytic opportunities. By its slanting orientation to conventional discourses, the non-imitative potential of such an address may open important lines of thinking about the goals and tactics of educational study—complicating rather than confirming spaces for doing critical work.

The Rhizomatic

The address of the rhizomatic recodes a method of literary analysis enacted by Gilles Deleuze and Félix Guattari in their study of the writing of Franz Kafka.[27] Initially confronting the question, "How can we enter into Kafka's work?"[28] Deleuze and Guattari develop a method of analytic experimentation—one that immediately "detach[es] Kafka" from categorical methodologies which have traditionally organized analysis of his art through any one of a number of conventional theoretical systems: symbolism, dialectics, psychoanalytics, myth, etc.—methodologies which lead "precisely to failure: an always excessive reduction of his work."[29] Likening Kafka's art to "a rhizome, a burrow"—a virtually endless, complex, densely connected series of structures and interstructures with multiple entrances, galleries, intersections, dead ends, main and side doors,[30] Deleuze and Guattari bring to the surface of their critical writing a strategics of methodological reversal:

> We will enter, then, by any point whatsoever; none matters more than another, and no entrance is more privileged even if it seems an impasse, a tight passage, a siphon. We will be trying only to discover what other points our entrance connects to, what crossroads and

galleries one passes through to link two points, what the map of the rhizome is and how the map is modified if one enters by another point. Only the principle of multiple entrances prevents the introduction of the enemy, the Signifier, and those attempts to interpret a work that is actually only open to experimentation. [31]

Thus, for Deleuze and Guattari the process of critical practice related to Kafka's art is not to explain what it is or to determine its absolute meaning through the recuperation of carefully selected points of data that are hierarchically organized to prove specific truths within a single, predetermined theoretical category—but rather to open up new ways of extracting from this "expression machine" (a given artwork) its intensities, tonalities, and energy. [32]

Although Deleuze and Guattari's analytic was originally constructed for specific readings of the work of Franz Kafka, it is worth the effort, I think, to experiment with folding this criticality across conceptual realms and to explore its parallel applications. Thus, the effort to recode it as a mode of address here. Considered in this way, Deleuze and Guattari's analytic provides a tactical methodology that undermines compartmentalized systems of educational study, unlocking discussion of the nominal subject from the hold of top-down reasoning and categorizing practice. In effect, inquiry about the nature of these artistic projects can become freed from the restrictions of a belief exercise—that of assembling an "explanation" of their meaning in relation to a given theory. What becomes possible instead is the creation of a provisional analytic field that provides for these artistic projects' multiple affirmations, pursues and/or mirrors their shifting energies, and defers any final positioning of their artistic and cultural status.

Such an address produces the potential for a really interesting writing and reading practice. By bringing into discursive play the idea of a work of art as a rhizomatic assembly of densely entangled crossroads, passages, galleries, and heterogeneities, complemented by the method of multiple analytic stances ("We will enter, then, by any point whatsoever; none matters more than another, and no entrance is more privileged even if it seems an impasse…"), Deleuze and Guattari's method interferes with—and ultimately frustrates—the construction of a writing that produces a *unanimous reading* of an art work's status. Pulsing with the energies of categorical reversal, such a mode of address sets into motion possibilities for encoding a writing that produces an *uneven reading*—a reading that angles away from the conventions of reading, since its recognitions of the subject always seem to be mediated by other versions of that subject, always seem to be opening to multiple acknowledgments and displacements, always seem to be layered and layering, always seem to be escaping through other entrances, galleries, and passages—depending upon a single shift of perspective. [33]

Although such a mode of address might initially provoke questions about analytic "slippage" from formal perspectives, Deleuze and Guattari consider such issues to be "low-intensity," since these concerns move thinking to return, in their view, to the formulaic, the predictable. The "threshold" issue, as Deleuze and Guattari point out, is always that of analytic invention, or gambling—for, as they observe, "art is a mirror, which goes 'fast,' like a watch—sometimes."[34]

The construction, organization, and enactment of an analytic strategy inscribing these multiple modes of address is a move that consciously attempts to both affirm and contribute to the developing critical discourse that explores the multiple ways that meaning can be represented while avoiding methods of address that, in their exclusiveness and singularity, might well reflect oppressive theoretical and procedural approaches. Linking these modes of address to the projects of study in this book thus generates a forum for a series of enunciations that are normally not found in official educational discourses. In their non-sequential improvisations, indirections, and visual reference, these enunciations denote a particular kind of inquiry—one that shifts attention to a criticality funded by multiple representations of educationally configured realities, and in so doing, opens spaces for what Gregory Ulmer has identified as "post-criticism": "a hybrid of literature and criticism, art and science" where "knowledge of an object of study may be obtained without conceptualization or explanation."[35] Such criticism, Ulmer points out in referencing statements by Jacques Derrida related to the experimental in textual inscription, "proves without showing, without evidencing any conclusion, without entailing anything, without an available thesis. It proves according to a different mode...."[36]

Despite the valuations provoked by this kind of critical stance, issues related to its implementation can not be considered above concern. The fundamentally independent nature of its structure is certainly vulnerable to accusation from specific communities. Its indirections and spatial proportions invite straight-line ideological interrogation. The determination to chart an analytic course deliberately located at a slant to official narratives of educational power interrupts, for example, the ideals of any kind of cohesive politics in the traditional sense. Moreover, the various modes of address described above offer no centralized agenda grounded in the mechanics of "a close reading" of conventional, structural materialities that directs thinking to a universal, liberal goal of social change. Dispersing the political (and the conventional mechanics of its expression) from the privilege of a central analytic position and situating its language along with (and/or within) other language systems may be viewed as problematic, since such an approach could easily be interpreted as tacitly supporting the status quo, recirculating conservative strategies that solidify unjust power relations.

Are these concerns warranted? Are other readings of these criticisms possible? While it could be argued that these criticisms provide their own best response, I found it useful to gain a different perspective on these issues from another standpoint, but one that highlights similar difficulties.

In the concluding chapter of her book reappraising the relationship of Michel Foucault's work to feminist theory and practice, Jana Sawicki borrows the term "risky" to discuss the implications of certain apolitical tendencies in Foucault's discourse that are problematic for feminism. This useful term—and Sawicki's careful comments related to its implications for critical work—may be pondered with reference to the analytic strategies charted in this project. She writes:

> Risky practices are those about which there is conflicting evidence concerning their practical and political implications. There are good reasons to adopt them and good reasons to doubt them. In other words, calling practices risky implies that although there is no hard and fast evidence that they lead to or perpetuate relations of domination, there is also sufficient reason to question them.[37]

But as Sawicki also notes several pages later, risky practice is plural in dimension. There is also the risk that Foucault saw in "becoming too comfortable" with the certainties of one's own positions, one's truths, one's theories and assumptions about how the world works, and one's requirements in it.[38] She includes Teresa de Lauretis's observation (with reference to feminist theory) that often what is required is

> leaving or giving up a place that is safe, that is "home"—physically, emotionally, linguistically, epistemologically—for another place that is unknown and risky, that is not only emotionally but conceptually other; a place of discourse from which speaking and thinking are at best tentative, uncertain, unguaranteed.[39]

Although de Lauretis and Sawicki are clearly writing from the felt requirements of different theoretical and practical necessities, I found in their words a strong and powerful borrowing that sustained the idea of an ongoing requirement to test out and work through alternate analytic stances. From this perspective, and put another way, choosing not to explore forms of thinking that are "tentative, uncertain, unguaranteed" contains powerful elements of its own kind of risky practice, and putting closure to the possibilities of alternative inquiry in educational study can serve as an equally powerful vehicle for affirming the status quo.

———————

To take risks then, to test critical limits, to make "bold omissions."[40]

To find pleasure in experimenting with the stabilities of language in order to repoliticize the status of inquiry by which current bodies of knowledge are represented/produced.

Can such an approach open to encouraging terrain?
Can a writing that relates to what gives no conventional return alter thinking about analytic relations?
Or will it only reproduce the pyramids all over again?

NOTES

The epigraph for this chapter is taken from Maxine Greene, "Blue Guitars and the Search for Curriculum," in *Reflections from the Heart of Educational Inquiry: Understanding Curriculum and Teaching Through the Arts*, eds. George Willis and William H. Schubert (Albany: SUNY Press, 1991), p. 122.

1. Jean Fisher, "Tim Rollins + Kids of Survival," *Artforum*, (January 1987), p. 111.

2. Cameron McCarthy, "Marxist Theories of Education and the Challenge of a Cultural Politics of Non-Synchrony," in *Becoming Feminine: The Politics of Popular Culture*, eds. Leslie Roman and Linda Christian-Smith with Elizabeth Ellsworth (Philadelphia: The Falmer Press, 1988), p. 200.

3. Elizam Escobar, "Art of Liberation: A Vision of Freedom," in *Reimaging America: The Arts of Social Change*, eds. Mark O'Brien and Craig Little (Philadelphia: New Society Publishers, 1990), p. 86.

4. See, for example, Elizabeth Ellsworth, "Why Doesn't This Feel Empowering? Working Through the Repressive Myths of Critical Pedagogy," *Harvard Educational Review*, Vol. 59, No. 3 (August 1989), pp. 297–324; Trinh T. Minh-ha, *When the Moon Waxes Red: Representation, Gender, and Cultural Politics* (New York: Routledge, 1991), and *Woman, Native, Other: Writing Postcoloniality and Feminism* (Bloomington: Indiana University Press, 1989); Patti Lather, *Getting Smart: Feminist Research and Pedagogy With/in the Postmodern* (New York: Routledge, 1991); and Janice Jipson, Petra Munro, Susan Victor, Karen Jones, and Gretchen Rowland, *Positions on Imposition: Multiple Cultural Realities* (Westport, Connecticut: Bergin & Garvey, forthcoming).

5. Richard Rorty, "Self-creation and affiliation: Proust, Nietzsche, and Heidegger," *Contingency, irony, and solidarity* (New York: Cambridge University Press, 1989), p. 96.

6. A personal and very much abbreviated list of sources here includes:

On Postmodernism: Steven Connor, *Postmodernist Culture: An Introduction to Theories of the Contemporary* (London: Basil Blackwell, 1989); Jean-François Lyotard, *The Postmodern Condition: A Report on Knowledge* (Minneapolis: University of Minnesota Press, 1984); Michel Foucault, *Language, Counter-Memory, Practice: Selected Essays and Interviews*, ed. Donald Bouchard (Ithaca: Cornell University Press, 1977); *Discourses: Conversations in Postmodern Art and Culture*, eds. Russell Ferguson, William Olander, Marcia Tucker, and Karen Fiss (Cambridge: MIT Press, and New York: The New Museum of Contemporary Art, 1990).

On Feminism: Toril Moi, *Sexual/Textual Politics: Feminist Literary Theory* (New York: Routledge, 1988); Hélène Cixous and Catherine Clément, *The Newly Born Woman* (Minneapolis: University of Minnesota Press, 1986); Trinh T. Minh-ha, *When the Moon Waxes Red* and *Woman, Native, Other*; Rachel Blau DuPlessis, *The Pink Guitar: Writing as Feminist Practice* (New York: Routledge, 1990); Nancy K. Miller, *Getting Personal: Feminist Occasions and Other Autobiographical Acts* (New York: Routledge, 1991).

7. Carol Becker, *Social Responsibility and the Place of the Artist in Society* (Chicago: Lake View Press, 1990), p. 13. This wording is from Becker's response to the questions: "What *is* the place of art in American society? What *is* the place of the artist?" While her extended answer presents a complicated, problematic overview of the issue, the initial sentence of her response begins: "In the nineteenth century, American writers, Walt Whitman, Melville, and others, had a vision of the artist-writer in America as the voice of democracy, integral to the daily life of a pluralistic society, representing diverse, hidden, necessary points of view." By deliberately integrating these objectives— the representation of "diverse, hidden, necessary points of view"—into the framework of this writing project, I acknowledge a crucial historical connection, as well as the imperative of

resituating these questions across category (education) and time (this present, this now).

8. Nancy K. Miller, *Getting Personal*, p. 75. Miller cites Mary Jacobus in the development of a politics of writing and difference that resists hierarchy. As Miller observes: "*We could also think of this juxtaposition as an exercise in feminist intertextualities; a process of reading through, rather than towards, that Mary Jacobus describes in* Reading Woman *as* 'correspondences': its 'itinerary incomplete and... destination deferred' (292); a choreography of bodies on the move, sometimes in synch, more often, in collision.*" Miller's italics.

9. See, for example, *Reflections from the Heart of Educational Inquiry*; Maxine Greene, *Landscapes of Learning* (New York: Teachers College Press, 1978); and Eliot Eisner, *The Educational Imagination* (New York: Macmillan, 1979). For the particular wording of this question, I am indebted to Rosalyn Deutsche, who, in an essay on a series of exhibitions organized by the Dia Art Foundation exploring issues of art as it moves into the urban sphere, asked: "How is the city an issue for art?" in "Alternative Space," in *If You Lived Here: The City in Art, Theory, and Social Activism*, ed. Brian Wallis (Seattle: Bay Press, 1991), p. 46.

10. Maxine Greene, *Landscapes of Learning*, p. 173.

11. Trinh T. Minh-ha, "The Other Censorship," *When The Moon Waxes Red*, p. 232.

12. Recently, Robert Donmoyer has articulated the need for exploring what he has termed "artistic modes of data display" as a crucial issue in contemporary educational study. To pursue the differential possibilties of this criticality (as expressed in the various domains of performance, drama, music, and the visual and literary arts), Donmoyer is considering "artistic modes of data display" as a thematic for what he is planning as the first in a series of annual conferences exploring issues related to curriculum, art, and educational study. (Personal conversation, May 6, 1993, Washington, D.C.).

See also, for example, Hayden White's recommendations (in writing the history of literature) as noted by Gregory Ulmer, and Ulmer's articulation for their elaboration across disciplines to develop a transformative criticality (a "post-criticism") grounded in the strategies of contemporary artistic practice. In developing the framework for such a criticism, Ulmer follows White's suggestion to explore "the possibility of using impressionistic, expressionistic, surrealistic, and (perhaps) even actionist modes of representation for dramatizing the significance of data which [researchers] have uncovered but which all too frequently they are prohibited from seriously contemplating as evidence...." Hayden White, *Tropics of Discourse* (Baltimore: Johns Hopkins University Press, 1978), pp. 42, 47–48; quoted in Gregory L. Ulmer, "The Object of Post-Criticism," in *The Anti-Aesthetic: Essays on Postmodern Culture*, ed. Hal Foster (Port Townsend, Washington: Bay Press, 1983), p. 83.

13. Jill Godmilow, "Far from Finished: Deconstructing the Documentary," (An interview by Brooke Jacobson), in *Reimaging America*, p. 181.

14. This recognition draws upon and repeats Rachel Blau DuPlessis's observation of her own experiments with an uncontained critical writing practice. She writes: "The multiple pressures of living out feminist thinking led me again and again to this non-objective, polyvocal prose, whose writing I experienced as the most pleasure when it became most speculative and most uncontainable, most meditative and most passionate." *The Pink Guitar*, p. vii.

15. Walker Percy, "The Man on the Train," *The Message in the Bottle: How Queer Man Is, How Queer Language Is, and What One Has to Do with the Other* (New York: Farrar, Straus and Giroux, 1978), p. 91.

16. This, from Dick Hebdige's excellent overview of bricolage in *Subculture: The Meaning of Style.* (London: Methuen, 1979), pp. 102–106.

17. Chris Baldick, *The Concise Oxford Dictionary of Literary Terms* (Oxford: Oxford University Press, 1990), p. 26.

18. Some of the observations that follow here owe much to Oscar Kenshur's reading of Umberto Eco's notions of discontinuity, openness, and spatial form expressed in Eco's much revised essay, "The Poetics of the Open Work." Oscar Kenshur, *Open Form and the Shape of Ideas* (Cranbury, New Jersey: Associated University Presses, 1986). I am especially indebted to Kenshur's thinking on pp. 14–19.

19. Nancy K. Miller, *Getting Personal*, p. 75. See note in 8 above. Also see Trinh T. Minh-ha, *Framer Framed* (New York: Routledge, 1992).

20. Trinh T. Minh-ha, "Un-writing/Inmost Writing," *When the Moon Waxes Red*, p. 142. This citation, as Trinh notes, is Marshall McLuhan's, where he describes the nature of an auditory space characteristic of tribal cultures. She uses McLuhan's wording in talking about the multiform, shapeshifting *writerly spaces* constructed by Hélène Cixous and Clarice Lispector: "Forming, deforming, informing, malformed, many forms.... Perhaps life appears less agonizing when decentralization (and decentering) are no longer understood as chaos or absence—the opposite of presence—but as a marvelous expansion, a multiplicity of independent centers. Such an understanding can allow us, following Clarice Lispector's example, not to succumb to the need for form, linked to the terror of finding oneself without boundaries." (*Moon*, pp. 142–143).

21. Edward W. Said, "Opponents, Audiences, Constituencies and Community," in *The Anti-Aesthetic*, pp. 157–8. Said, acknowledging the usefulness of Peter Berger's thinking related to the incorporation of the visual in critical work, refers especially to the practice of photomontage.

22. Rachel Blau DuPlessis, *The Pink Guitar*, p. 163.

23. See, for example, Judith Barry, ed. Iwona Blazwick, *Public Fantasy* (London: Institute of Contemporary Arts, 1991); Trinh T. Minh-ha, *Framer Framed* ; Karen Finley, *Shock Treatment* (San Francisco: City Lights Books, 1992); Jacques Derrida, *Glas* (Lincoln: University of Nebraska Press, 1986). For groundbreaking earlier work, see John Cage, *Silence* (Middletown, Connecticut: Wesleyan University Press, 1961) and *A Year From Monday* (Middletown, Connecticut: Wesleyan University Press, 1969).

24. Patti Lather, *Getting Smart*, p. 91.

25. Trinh T. Minh-ha, "Bold Omissions," *When the Moon Waxes Red*, p. 161.

26. Trinh T. Minh-ha, "The Other Censorship," *When the Moon Waxes Red*, p. 230.

27. Gilles Deleuze and Félix Guattari, *Kafka: Toward a Minor Literature* (Minneapolis: University of Minnesota Press, 1986).

28. *Ibid.*, p. 3

29. *Ibid.*, p. xiv.

30. *Ibid.*, p. 3.

31. *Ibid.*

32. *Ibid.*, pp. 3–8, 28–42. Specific reference to the term "expression machine" is found on p. 28.

33. *Ibid.*, p. xxiv. I build here on their ideas of a "nomadic writing."

34. *Ibid.*, p. 28. Deleuze and Guattari bring forward this quote from Gustave Janouch, *Conversations with Kafka* (London: Andre Deutsch, 1971), p. 68.

35. Gregory L. Ulmer, "The Object of Post-Criticism," in *The Anti-Aesthetic*, p. 94.

36. *Ibid.*, pp. 93, 94. The quote is from (Ulmer notes) Derrida, *La Carte postale* (Paris: Flammarion, 1980), p. 317. Ulmer also references (pp. 93, 94) Derrida's creation of a critical writing in "Cartouches" in *The Truth in Painting* (Chicago: The University of Chicago Press, 1987), pp. 183–253. In this text, Jacques Derrida seeks to "talk about" an artistic work (*The Pocket-Size Tlingit Coffin* by Gerard Titus-Carmel, a kind of sculpture and an extended series of drawings of it, each drawing done from a different perspective) by producing "a discourse above, to one side of or below" (*Truth*, p. 190) the work(s), "turn[ing] them

round in all directions through a series of deviations, variations, modulations, anamorphoses. And then stop at a given moment (twenty pages more or less), in an apparently arbitrary fashion, as he [Titus-Carmel] did at the end of the year, more or less, in the mode of contingency" (*Truth*, p. 200).

37. Jana Sawicki, *Disciplining Foucault: Feminism, Power and the Body* (New York: Routledge, 1991), 102–3.

38. *Ibid.*, p. 107.

39. *Ibid.* Sawicki quotes from Teresa de Lauretis, "Eccentric Subjects: Feminist Theory and Historical Consciousness," *Feminist Studies*, Vol. 16, No. 1 (Spring 1990), p. 138.

40. Trinh T. Minh-ha, "Bold Omissions and Minute Depictions," *When the Moon Waxes Red*, pp. 155–168.

2

Tim Rollins + K.O.S.

Tim Rollins + K.O.S. (Nelson Savinon and Victor Llanos) working in the studio on *The Scarlet Letter*

"Everyone is Welcome"

FOR MORE THAN A DECADE, SOME OF THE MOST INTRIGUING activities in teaching and learning have come out of an independent workshop moving from space to space in the Hunts Point section of the South Bronx in New York City. It is in this workshop that Tim Rollins and Kids of Survival—an artist/teacher and a group of inner-city teenagers—make paintings on the pages of books, reshape forms of educational practice, and produce some of contemporary culture's most startling representations.

Rollins and his students work in an area of New York where over sixty percent of young people do not finish high school; where more than forty percent of the households are on welfare; where ninety-five percent of the population is "minority"; and where violence is an everyday occurrence because of the drug, prostitution, and gang economies.[1] Kids of Survival, or K.O.S., is a semi-changing group of adolescents who gave themselves their own title. Most of them are black and Puerto Rican youth, and most come from a part of New York so consistently represented in the media as marked by abandonment, poverty, and evaporated dreams that their urban landscape has long been considered the "ground zero" of American social policy.[2]

Rollins came to New York in 1975 from Maine, with an interest in art-making and teaching. From 1976-80, he pursued formal artistic and educational study, earning a B.F.A. from the School of Visual Arts and a master's degree in art education from New York University. During this time (in 1979), he also co-founded Group Material, an artists' collective that linked its artistic practice to issues of social, cultural, and political advocacy.

In mid-1981, Rollins was recruited to teach art classes at I.S. 52 to students classified as "learning-disabled," "dyslexic," "emotionally handicapped," and "neurologically brain-impaired."[3] Impressed by the number of his special education students who demonstrated artistic aptitude, Rollins transformed his classroom into a studio for making art.[4] In doing so, he also transformed his own ideas of what it meant to be an artist and a teacher. As he put it:

> I ceased being an artist who taught, and collapsed my artistic and teaching practices into one strange and stumbling hybrid. I made my art with the kids—during classes, during free periods, during lunch periods, in the short time after school allowed us before getting kicked out by the custodians.[5]

In 1982, Rollins established K.O.S. and the Art and Knowledge Workshop to accomodate this unique approach to pedagogy and art-making. Its initial base of operations was Room 318 in I.S. 52 where Rollins taught during the school day. Three years later, Rollins extended the idea further. Feeling constrained by the limitations of public-school time schedules, overcrowded classrooms, and hierarchies of bureaucratic control, he turned the Workshop into a non-profit, after-school organization, moving it into a gymnasium of an abandoned school on Longwood Avenue that had been refurbished as a neighborhood community center.[6] The Art and Knowledge's current (1993) location is the 9,000-square-foot third floor of an old factory building on Barretto Street, just south of the Bruckner Expressway. In this shifting series of alternative spaces, Rollins and K.O.S. have collaborated to explore, through the study of works of literary distinction and through art making, many of the complex social, political, and ideological factors which shape their daily lives in the South Bronx.

In an early writing, Rollins has spoken about the kinds of issues or "matters" with which he and K.O.S. wrestle in their workshop activity: to learn what actually interests them; to represent themselves directly and sincerely; and to confront the political and economic factors which determine their lives.[7] Working through these issues, Rollins and K.O.S. have evolved a pedagogy that is multifaceted, incorporating tactics from classical and radical, group and individual, personal and

K.O.S. working in the studio. Left top: Nelson Savinon; Left center: Victor Llanos, Carlos Rivera;
Left lower: Nelson Savinon, Victor Llanos; Mid center: Jorge Abreu, Jamel Lewis

from

the text

to the

threshold

Study on book page for *Amerika*, 1987   Courtesy Mary Boone Gallery

social sources. Generally the process begins with Rollins' selecting for group study a literary work that he thinks might—in whole or in part—interest his students and speak to matters that concern them. Not surprisingly, many of the works selected portray young adults as central characters. Some of the books read by the group in the past ten years include Lewis Carroll's *Through the Looking Glass*, Stephen Crane's *The Red Badge of Courage*, Nathaniel Hawthorne's *The Scarlet Letter*, Herman Melville's *Moby Dick*, Alex Haley's *The Autobiography of Malcolm X*, Carlo Collodi's *Pinocchio*, and Franz Kafka's *Amerika*.

Rollins and K.O.S. go through these books together, with Rollins either reading the selection out loud to the group or with members working from their own versions of the text. During these collaborative sessions, they discuss ideas and themes in the text as seem pertinent to them and develop possible connections between these themes and text/life situations. These working sessions and conversations are sometimes recorded. Sometimes before, sometimes during, and sometimes after these collaborative readings, members of K.O.S. make hundreds of small drawings (a process they call "jamming") which link aspects of the narrative with the realities of their daily existence. These drawings reflect a wide variety of sources: their workshop study in art history, their knowledge of popular culture, their visits to local museums, and their knowledge of current events and city and global politics. These drawings are not literal illustrations of the text(s); rather, they function as concentrated visual emblems and signs of the written work(s). A number of these images may then be painted as studies directly onto book pages.

The Art and Knowledge Workshop library and study area

Eventually, all these visual representations are collected and a set of the most "sincere and moving" images is arrived at through group discussion; this process can take months or years. The images are then transferred to transparencies and, through the use of an overhead projector, displayed onto a base of pages which have been torn from the book they have just read. In this way they arrange a composition for a large painting. As Rollins explains: "The book, something that one supposes we consume, has been converted into a work of art active with social uses, pertinent and concrete for us today."[8]

One of the most illuminating examples of how this pedagogy works is provided by Rollins and K.O.S.'s initial (1984–85) reading of Franz Kafka's *Amerika*—a work that would eventually generate the extended series of paintings for which they have become most well known. Rollins has explained his reasons for selecting a book by an author who, to some, might appear totally unsuitable for a group of inner-city teenagers:

> Kafka's text is perfect for us. Basically the plot is about a sixteen-year-old boy named Karl, who emigrates to New York and America to find, as always, fame and fortune. What Karl finds instead in this country is a unique Kafkaesque combination of reality and fantasy—a perception that a majority of children here seem to share (especially those who have just arrived from Puerto Rico).[9]

What was of particular interest in Kafka's book, however, was its final chapter, "The Nature Theatre of Oklahoma."

Rollins tells the story this way:

> At the end of the year, [Karl's] ready to go home. He says to himself, "I can't handle it, I'm a failure, I can't make it in Amerika." And so just as he's about ready to get back on the boat and go home, he hears this sound. It sounds like a Salvation Army band. They're all carrying these placards. And the placards say, "Come join the Nature Theatre of Oklahoma! The Nature Theatre of Oklahoma where anyone can be an artist and everyone is welcome!" And Karl looks at this and thinks, "I have been lied to, I have been cheated, I have been robbed, and I am sure this is just another situation where I'm going to get ripped off. But then again, that one sign says 'Everyone is welcome.' Even if it is bullshit, I'm going to try it. I've never seen that in Amerika before." So he joins.
>
> Then they say, "Well, we're leaving for Clayton tonight on a train. We're all going to go at midnight, so you've got to get registered at the racetrack. You have to register before midnight because that's when the train goes, and you lose your chance forever." So he goes to the racetrack, and as he approaches the racetrack, he hears this incredible sound of a traffic jam, and it's hundreds of horns like a jazz orchestra or something. And as he walks into the racetrack he sees an incredible scene of hundreds of people standing on pedestals, dressed up like angels blowing whatever they want to on these long golden horns. There's a big

Amerika I, 1984–85   Courtesy Mary Boone Gallery

fat person who's making little noises, and a little skinny person making big noises, and it's this big kind of mess. All these sounds together.

And Karl asks the old man who brings him in, "What is this?" and the guy says, "This is Amerika, where everyone has a voice and everyone can say what they want." That's it. Then I say [to K.O.S.], "Now look, you all have your own taste and you have different voices. If you could be a golden instrument, if you could play a song of your freedom and dignity and your future and everything you feel about Amerika and this country, what would your horn look like?"[10]

As Rollins recalls, K.O.S.'s response was startling, explosive. They crafted their own versions of Kafka's golden horns. They made small, intricate horns; curving and straight horns; and horns that looked energetic, vigorous, and extravagant. They made horns that seemed recognizable and horns that appeared to have no reference to any known reality. Eventually, a selected number of these images were shaped into a large composition painted onto every single one of Kafka's 298 pages, which Rollins had adhered to a six-by-fifteen foot ground of heavyweight rag paper.

The result of their work is *Amerika I*, completed in March of 1985. A painting of dazzling visual expressiveness, majestic proportion, and subtle complexity, it pulses with multiple meanings that shuttle across category and time. From one standpoint, *Amerika I* suggests intriguing textual associations extending beyond the narrative realities of the book, in that

what

is

this

voice

IT IS OTHER WORLDLY AND THIS-WORLDLY, OF DAYS LONG GONE AND OF THIS VERY DAY, AN ANTIQUITY WITHOUT DATES. HERETICAL AND DEVOUT, INNOCENT AND PERVERTED, LIMPID AND MURKY, AERIAL AND SUBTERRANEAN, OF THE HERMITAGE AND OF THE CORNER BAR, WITHIN HAND'S REACH AND ALWAYS BEYOND.

the painting's opulence could easily pass for a visual representation of Kafka's rhetorical style. The interconnected groups of meticulous, intricately painted trumpets, for example, make one think of Kafka's own obsessive, cramped, precisely crafted tangle of sentences, while the fantastically shaped horns recall his eccentric depiction of an impossible reality. Even the heroic size of the painting, with its dominant golden hue, acts to reinforce Kafka's imagined view of the New World (he never visited America) as a place of "almost limitless theater," wealth, and glittering promise.

From another perspective, *Amerika I* suggests connections

Amerika VI, 1986–87   Courtesy Mary Boone Gallery

TIM [ROLLINS]: Is there any unity in our work?

GEORGE [GARCES]: I think all the pieces look different.

TIM: But what about a meaning or mood that connects all this new work?

RICHARD [CRUZ]: Well, I know it's not a happy mood!

GEORGE: When we started, it was real important to make beautiful things like the golden horns in the *Amerika* paintings, the *Scarlet Letter* works, but these new things don't get lost in beauty.

RICHARD: We're not making the paintings that people want us to.

NELSON [MONTES]: We can't be making those golden horns forever!

TIM: We could be millionaires! (Laughter)

NELSON: The way I see it, the older work was more about freedom. The new work is about being trapped.

K.O.S. working in studio on *The Scarlet Letter*

with a wide variety of artistic traditions: 1980s practices of appropriation; the politics of surrealism and collage; the collective productions of William Morris and notions related to the "beautiful" in art; visual references to illuminated manuscripts; the muralist histories of Latin and South America; medieval tapestries; and the heroic veils of abstract expressionist painting.

From still another point of view, *Amerika I* is charged with political energies: its tangled, interlocking chaos of golden horns—each carefully fashioned to articulate a message of personal liberty—presents a compelling statement from the urban landscape of the South Bronx to contemporary American society. Read in this way, Rollins and K.O.S.'s *Amerika I* is active with urgent meaning. It presents, in very concrete terms, a unified image that glitters with a singular and collective message of liberty to the wider social structure—an image that, as Rollins notes, is both "beautiful and dangerous" at the same time.

From yet one more position, but not finally, *Amerika I* can be read as objective evidence of a heterodox pedagogical process at work. This approach honors the traditions of the academy—scholarship, analysis, the book, dialogue, collaboration—but it can also be seen as the embodiment of its radical transformation. This transformation suggests connections with Freirian notions of education as a form of cultural politics. In this framework, teachers and students mutually engage in a series of investigations whose focus is to critically examine and scrutinize forms of contemporary culture as part of the broader social task of constructing the material realities of a more just and democratic life.

Since this initial *Amerika* painting, there have been more than a dozen subsequent versions (as of this writing), each done by a semi-changing group of students. Most of these paintings link Kafka's text to the realities of students' lives in New York, and many suggest a less optimistic stance than others. *Amerika VI*, for example, with its massive uppercase letters, "H" and "B", serving as parameters for the painting, call to mind the divisive events of Howard Beach in the borough of Queens that took place in December of 1986 (or, as Rollins has related, "They also signify the name Hieronymus Bosch and the netherworld this artist represents."[11]) In fact, Rollins indicates that the painting was a social mediation, done as a memorial to the racial incident that took place there. Still, there's a sense that this *Amerika* might be a visual reference for the actualities of confinement, enclosure. K.O.S.'s horns of liberty seem to be entangled within a grid-like assembly that resembles a fence, a barrier, or a cage of golden bars.

Rollins and K.O.S. have also transformed Stephen Crane's *The Red Badge of Courage* into a series of paintings which cross similar spatial and conceptual ground. *The Red Badge of Courage III*, for example, measuring six by eleven feet, suggests both the panorama of a Civil War battlefield and a stylized aerial view of a city neighborhood. The scores of pages torn from the book and attached side by side onto canvas order the text into seemingly endless linear arrangement—an abstract compositional device that evokes images of hundreds of troop regiments or a grid of innumerable city streets and blocks on a map. Moreover, the scores of jewel-like punctures that scar

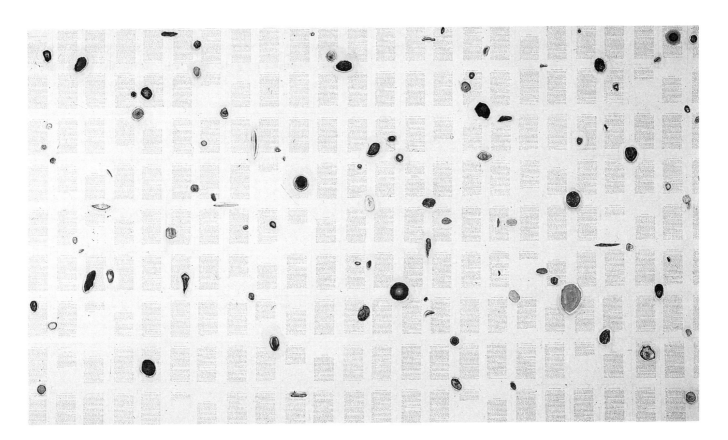

By Any Means Necessary, 1965, 1986   Courtesy Mary Boone Gallery

the surface of the painting and "eat into it like wounds"[12] serve as a powerful reminder not merely of the horror of a distant Civil War but also of how the lives of youth are so repeatedly appropriated and expended throughout history by an adult community ever eager to advance its own political ideologies. (Recently, Rollins has explained that the imagery in "The Red Badge of Courage" series was in many ways inspired by the scars on the bodies of several of his students; the series is largely about these wounds—or "badges of courage"—and also about surviving in the South Bronx despite the daily threats of violence.[13])

In a 1986 version of *By Any Means Necessary*, painted after reading *The Autobiography of Malcolm X*, a simpler image and smaller size prevail. Two scalpel-like, crossing lines are richly drawn in black-on-white book pages which have been attached to a twenty-one by twenty-eight-inch sheet of linen. The image is powerful and conceptually incisive: cutting across the whiteness of the text, it can be read as a "stylized M and X [that] intersect one another like a monogram and could easily pass [for] a logo...."[14] But a monogram and logo of what? Is this stylization a visual signature or a stamp of cancellation? A mark of identification or an emblem of censorship? A reference for a person or a symbol for something X-rated? Or is the image's abruptly altered linearity suggestive of something else altogether? A signal, perhaps, for vectors in conflict that call to mind the complex, problematic course of Malcolm X's life itself? Read in this way, the slope of one line, while briefly interrupted by momentary decline, is positive overall; the direction of the other, however, pointed-

Everybody asks why

it's black [*Black Alice*]. I thought black was a
good color, especially for the Eighties. So many
girls suffered. They got pregnant too young, they
feel trapped, they start young and get confused
and then the big problems come.

—Annette Rosado, K.O.S.

ly charts an unabbreviated, precipitous fall. Rather than establishing any conclusive answers to these questions, K.O.S.'s reinterpretation of *The Autobiography of Malcolm X* provides opportunities to think through the kinds of identities, knowledges, and forms of progress that are most honored in American culture, and those which are censored and cancelled out.

In *Black Alice*, one of Rollins and K.O.S.'s responses to Lewis Carroll's *Through the Looking Glass*, book pages are once again torn out, adhered to a large canvas, and then completely painted over in black. Within the blackened part of the painting, a full-size figure of a youth is dimly visible, seemingly trapped within the dark. It is the figure of Alice, also painted black (the subtle coloration drew on their study of the work of the American abstract painter Ad Reinhardt). Roberta Smith has noted meanings of struggle and resistance generated by this painting:

> The way the huge, barely visible figure is confined
> within the blackness of this surface is quite effective,
> both perceptually and as a metaphor for the conflict
> between personal growth and social inequity.[15]

Recognitions of this order suggest connections to political and ethical spheres—particularly when the rights of so many young girls in urban settings are repeatedly circumscribed by the legislative efforts of a right-thinking adult community on issues of reproduction, birth control, and sexuality. Seen this way, K.O.S.'s *Black Alice* evokes connections with the work of

literate

obliterate

devotion

devour

another contemporary artist, Barbara Kruger, who has deliberately used the phrase, "Your body is a battleground," as the textual leitmotif for a site-specific artwork addressing similar issues, albeit from a different perspective.[16]

But *Black Alice* yields still other recognitions. As one looks at the painting, the figure of Alice seems to alternately emerge from the background darkness or disappear into the void again. (A No where, Know where, Now where, Alice?)

"Seeing" where Alice "is" in K.O.S.'s transformation of Carroll's classic text challenges one's sense of sight visually and conceptually—where perception depends a great deal on the quality of the viewer's (social, personal, and political) attentiveness, position, and degree of critical investment. If one isn't a careful observer, *Black Alice* never exists at all. Out of anyone's time, she is maybe here or there or no place— opaque, matte, blackened out. This is a painting that moves back and forth across objective and conceptual locations: alternately a work of art and also an instrument that sharpens perception. *Black Alice* may well be a contemporary "Looking Glass" through which viewers can examine—not just notions about an artwork—but perhaps, much more subtly, recognitions about themselves.

In making these images which comment with conviction and subtlety on issues of presentation/representation, authority/autonomy, freedom/control, Rollins and K.O.S. generate a powerful series of questions related to the politics of cultural production. Who makes a culture's histories? Its systems of meanings? Its representations and mythologies?

Traditionally, tasks related to identifying, defining, and interpreting the various codes, themes, and meanings of a culture have been an occupation reserved for those individuals considered to possess the proper knowledge to do so. Broadly speaking, these individuals are routinely considered to be the adults of any given culture, and often those adults more specifically distinguished by class, gender, age, and color. Frequently acting to reproduce their own particular set of interests and values, this privileged group recirculates processes which often exclude the views and representations of other groups. Especially discounted in the heirarchies of cultural production are the views, issues, and methods of inquiry of children and youth of color and class in urban environments; the connection between their daily lives and the making of a society's cultural capital is one of almost total invisibility.

Jean Fisher, a London-based writer, describes exactly this situation in her discussion of Rollins and K.O.S.'s work and suggests how their partnership "radically challenge[s] these purist and elitist notions" regarding the mechanics of cultural production:

> K.O.S. begins with the book. Container of knowledge and guarantor of "civilized" culture, the book also represses those who are not its subjects, especially those educated in a history and ideology that effaces their own experiences and traditions. K.O.S., therefore, investigates classics of world literature, examining primary themes or instants in these texts that can be reinvested with K.O.S.'s knowledge and feelings, both of local experiences in the South Bronx as well as of

text	teach
book	breath
study	stain
myth	flesh
social	alien
transform	cancel
chapter	cipher
word	wound
statement	displacement
unity	scrutiny
academy	actuality
courage	cage
art	x
meaning	mutuality

broader world issues. The book is thus reclaimed. No longer merely an object of consumption, its pages form the ground upon which another image is constructed.[17]

By reclaiming the book from its previous set of historical interpretations and literary codifications, K.O.S. provides powerful resistance to many fixed cultural narratives, myths, and representations.

This complex process of cultural production/politics operates at yet another, more encompassing level. As Rollins has indicated, their transformation of books into art is "active with social uses." Compared to programs of traditional academic inquiry which rarely give students reason to connect their work with the forces of life outside the academy, Rollins and K.O.S. have forged links between their artistic/educational/cultural activities and institutional and cultural organizations in the larger social structure, demonstrating the valuable contributions young people can make to cultural interpretation. During the past decade, for example, Rollins and K.O.S.'s work has been widely exhibited in numerous settings at the local, state, national, and international levels. In conjunction with these exhibitions, Rollins and K.O.S. are frequently invited to speak about their work at museum and gallery openings. A recent instance involved Rollins and three members of K.O.S. (Nelson Savinon, Angel Abreu, and Victor Llanos) discussing their work at the Hirshhorn Museum of Art in Washington, D.C., where a monumental painting based on George Orwell's *Animal Farm* was displayed along with numerous supporting studies, as part of the museum's exhi-

Carlos Rivera, Victor Llanos working in the studio on *The Scarlet Letter*

bition series entitled "Directions." Further, institutions as diverse as The Museum of Modern Art, The Philadelphia Museum of Art, The Hirshhorn Museum, The Chase Manhattan Bank, and the Tate Gallery in London all own paintings by Rollins and K.O.S. These exhibitions and purchases have also generated an extensive and ongoing literature addressing their work and documenting its contribution and place in contemporary culture.

The work of Tim Rollins and K.O.S. moves across place, category, time. Its multiplicities include meanings in the art world, of course—but others, to repeat, can be pondered. From one perspective, their work extends conventional models of teaching and learning, animating the educational process with a radical political consciousness that is conspicuously absent from most formal educational settings. From another, their activity functions in a broader social sense, alternately reconstructing, reinterpreting, and offering resistance to many of the traditional themes, codes, and meanings articulated by the adult community. From yet another, their reading of literature functions as a challenge to conventional literary study and practice, since rather than being positioned as something fixed and read as an absolute, literature, for Rollins and K.O.S., is seen to play an active, mediating role between the past and the present, constantly needing to be reconsidered in the light of contemporary conditions and events. It is in some of these ways that their radical educational/artistic/cultural activities generate recognitions that unite students and history, art and experience, knowledge and culture, thereby making the past "pertinent and concrete for us today."

Carlos Rivera

Conversation with Tim Rollins and K.O.S.

Nick Paley: Let's begin by talking about how you arrive at choosing the books you use, and how you work together to transform them, to "read" them into art. **Nelson Savinon:** Most of the time Tim suggests the book. Then we sit around a table, like we are doing now, and Tim will explain the book and his ideas for it to us. There are some kids in K.O.S. who are dyslexic, so we read the book out loud to each other. We have a dialogue over a long period of time. Sometimes we record these talks. We talk about the book and how it relates to our lives now. In *The Red Badge of Courage* by Stephen Crane, this kid survives the Civil War. The relationship between this character in the book and us in K.O.S. is that we're surviving now in a society of constant, random violence—in a neighborhood where you can easily make so much money dropping out of school, standing on a corner selling drugs. Instead, we have decided to work our butts off and come to the studio and be artists. We have challenged fate and we are succeeding. Sometimes we come to the books by accident. Once, one of the kids came in, threw a paperback copy of *The Scarlet Letter* down on the table and yelled, "I *hate* this book!" He had to read it for a school assignment. And it was funny, because Tim said, "Oh, but *The Scarlet Letter* is one of the *great* books!" and on and on. It was later that we found out Tim had never read it! **Tim Rollins:** I'd never read *The Scarlet Letter*. Can you believe I got all the way to graduate school without having to read it? Still, I knew the book's reputation and was angry that the kid simply dismissed it. He said, "I can't understand it. It's so boring: all those 'thees' and 'thous'!" So I immediately waxed teacher-

ish and said, "But listen, this is *Hawthorne*. This is one of the greatest novels of American, if not world literature. How can it be boring? You're being barbaric…" and all that. So the kid counters with, "Then *you* help me understand it!" I hesitated a little; then I said, "Well, let me borrow your copy, and I'll read some of it at home tonight to refresh my memory of the story." On my way home on the Number Six train that night I started reading and, as you know, the book begins with this long, strange, circuitous and tedious introduction called "The Custom-House." And as I'm reading it, I couldn't help thinking, "Damn, the kid was right. This is slow going." But after this I finally hit the amazing first chapter, "The Prison-Door," just two pages, and I immediately knew this was one of the greatest books I had ever read. As for making paintings out of *The Scarlet Letter*, I didn't then know exactly what to do, but I did know that this book spoke clearly to us. I knew that the story of Hester was very much our story and the story of the South Bronx as well. To transform stigma into pride—this is the work of art. Hester's wearing of the "A" is more than punishment. She becomes a living model, a walking reminder, of the community's propensity towards sin. This is very similar to how the United States as a whole treats the South Bronx. Our neighborhood is a symbol for urban decay. The South Bronx is allowed to exist, especially for the media, but only as a model for suffering and decrepitude. Why? Because, like the crowds who scorned Hester, watching the violence of the Bronx on TV or in the papers makes everyone outside of the area feel good, safe, and secure in their places, in their values.

I think mass media, especially T.V., has made America this narrow, cruel, hypocritical and Puritan small town once again. **Angel Abreu:** If you are from the South Bronx, you wear a kind of "A" wherever you go. It's too bad. **Tim:** The idea to work with books, as the subjects *and* objects of our art came out of my everyday teaching experience in a junior high school on Kelly Street in the Bronx. I began art classes for the special-education department there, where most of the kids were evaluated as learning-disabled, dyslexic, emotionally handicapped, or neurologically impaired. First, most of my students couldn't physically read books. Second, even the kids who could read lacked the volition, the will to read anything but comic books. They had bought into that terrible ghetto myth that reading is for white people, that books are the enemy. I understand this sentiment, coming from a working-class family in rural Maine. At home, if you were a reader you were called a book-worm and that was pejorative. Books threaten. Why? I think first because books read you, they are a mirror that reflects your ignorance. And books are real intruders. They make you engage with a life-world beyond the strictures of your own home, family, and values. **Angel:** Where I come from, reading is often considered useless. Not practical. No one gets paid to read. What you get from books isn't tangible enough to be respected. **Tim:** Look, when you are brought up not to live decade to decade, or year to year, or even month to month—when you live day to day, then what you're going to eat for breakfast, then lunch, then dinner—these become the burning issues of your life—not what the "A" on Hester's breast represents. But I'm certain that

becoming involved with books—especially older novels—connects us with history in a way we can feel. Books relate the visceral struggle we undertake now with struggle from the past. I love where I come from, but the world I inherited felt too narrow for me—it pinched like a pair of shoes three sizes too small. I believe literature gives us a sense of history that makes living day-to-day cynical and ludicrous. Contrary to what many romantic journalists and academics might think, my working in the Bronx comes more from anger than altruism. I'm enraged and disgusted at how the institution of the school has given knowledge a bad reputation. In this context, you see, books become—literally—a battleground, not only for the images we paint on them, but for the clashing of issues that always seems to surround discussions of our work. For example, *The Scarlet Letter*, after working with its themes and pages for years now, doesn't just belong to comparative-lit students or a well-educated elite—it *belongs to us*. We have invaded the text so it visually, intellectually, practically makes sense to us. The novel becomes a teaching machine, and we enlist old Nathaniel Hawthorne to our cause in Hunts Point in 1992 and beyond. **Nick:** One of the things that strikes me about this entire process is that you are rescuing these works from historicity, their imprisonment in history, their forgottenness in time. You are bringing them to this time, this present, this place. **Tim:** We usually select books that need the dust blown off them. And we often get to a point in our discussions, in the work, where we ask, "What would Hawthorne think of this?" When we think the author would approve, that's when we release the paintings from the studio. **Nick:**

Has this process evolved or changed over the time you've been working together? Have you modified any aspects of the methodology of your book selection? **Nelson:** I don't know how to describe the process exactly. But if any of us has an idea about a book, we'll come into the studio and discuss it. But usually, Tim is always coming up with the books, and then later on we all sit around a table and discuss the possibilities of working with the text. Lots of times, Tim's ideas for books don't make any sense right away. **Tim:** I throw the ball out into the court, and it usually gets knocked around for a few years until a pattern of ideas emerges from the discussions—a group of images—possible images, a pattern—appears in our heads. Some game develops. The work starts flowing. Looking back, I think we have two basic styles of work. For example, in the "Amerika" works or "The Scarlet Letter" or "The Red Badge of Courage" paintings there is a ground—which is the text—and the kids and I come up with our own elements, like golden horns or red and gold "A"'s or mandala-like wounds that are then composed together and applied to the ground of bookpages. Like the music of John Cage, we are working with a structure that, in a way, cannot fail as a work of art. It's a democratic form and method—much like quilt-making. In these works the collaborative process is perhaps most apparent. But then we make works that cover the tracks of their making—*The Whiteness of the Whale* on Melville's *Moby Dick*, the "Black Beauty" and "Metamorphosis" paintings, the new "Pinocchio" sculptures or *From the Earth to the Moon* after Jules Verne. In these works the concept is arrived at collaboratively, but these pieces don't reveal any collective "touch."

Maybe our big challenge for our second decade is to integrate these two styles of work to create a third, deeper approach to collaboration—something more like a Baptist choir. **Nick:** It seems to me that there are some differences between the kind of teaching and learning that you do at the studio, and the teaching and learning that goes on in schools. Can you talk about that? **Nelson:** The teaching and learning in school is so different from how we work in the studio. In public school it's like you're in prison in a room with forty other people and you have to be there. The teachers, after so many years of doing the same thing, you can tell they are really bored. They write the aim of the day's lesson on the board, you copy it down and that's it. I've always felt that I learned more after school when I went to the studio. We have more resources. We have our own library. We learn a lot about historical references that we can put into our paintings. We get into geometry and math by calculating the sizes of the works. There's no boundaries to what we can learn. But school—it's a giant daycare center. Actually, you feel the real aim of going to school is just getting out. I'm talking about public high school now. College is so different. **Tim:** Nelson has just finished his first two weeks of art school. Free at last! **Nelson:** What I like about college is you educate yourself. It's up to you. **Angel:** Going to college is a big deal for our generation, coming from the South Bronx. It's a good feeling. **Nick:** How has the experience of working together over the past couple of years changed or affected your idea about education or school? **Angel:** It has given me the skills to work with other people. I'm not sure if I want to be a professional artist now, but I'm probably going to get into some profession where I can work with other people. Working with K.O.S. has helped me in this way. **Nick:** Nelson? **Nelson:** Before I joined the group, it was so hard for me to work and relate with people. I'm a really quiet person. I'm into myself. But when you're in the group, you have no choice but to work with the people in the group. I've been in the workshop seven years now. The process has become easier and easier for me through the years. When we make a work of art, we all agree so fast on a decision that it feels natural to us. We are so accustomed to working together. It's been such a long time. And now I'm thinking of becoming an art teacher. After this year, I may move into art education. Right now, the older members of K.O.S. are all considering becoming teachers, because we are taking on that role, working with the new and younger members of K.O.S. Like Victor may not know how to do something or have a question—so he comes up to me. I'm like his role model because I know where he's coming from. I come from there myself. **Tim:** For example, this morning Nelson was teaching Victor how to tie his tie. For years, that was always my job—one of the hardest duties. I was so busy rushing around this morning, preparing for the opening today, that it was great to have Nelson take over for me. **Nelson:** I'm beginning to understand what Tim went through with us all these years. **Tim:** Our working process has become very organic. As I began to see this happening, I became more intrigued with John Dewey's notion of the "organic intellectual." I feel that through our workshop, through our way of making art, learning comes naturally not so much from study but from occupation—a more active and engaged form of study. It now seems obvious that this is what our project has been aiming for all along. I've become invigorated by the American pragmatist tradition—Emerson, Thoreau, DuBois, William James, and Dewey—Cornel West, Rorty. More than, say Marx, Engels, and Brecht—these thinkers make more sense to me and our work right now—they make sense in the American grain—they make sense of the apparent chaos of the South Bronx and the U.S. as a whole. And I believe that the South Bronx now is more genuinely "American" than, say, the historic districts of Boston. There are many elements of America's future living in the South Bronx today. The idea fills some people with apprehension, some people with dread, and others with hope and joy. **Nick:** Tim, were you required to go through a teacher-education program? **Tim:** I took all my education classes studying for a master's in art education at New York University. So I took studio courses, sociology and history of education classes, theory, and those inane one-credit required courses like "Drug and Alcohol Education." I didn't quite finish because I had an opportunity to go to China to study cultural and educational institutions, so I left school early. When I returned I got my requirements together and entered the public-school system. **Nick:** If you had to identify those particular books and writers who have influenced your concept of teaching, who would those writers and what would those books be? **Tim:** Brecht's appendix to his great play, *Galileo*, called "Writing the Truth: Five Difficulties" is a source of constant inspiration to me. Also, the influence of Paolo Freire has been seminal to my ideas and work, especially that little monograph called "Cultural Action for Freedom" published by the Harvard Educational Review. Of course, the work and writings and attitude of Dr. Robert Coles helped me find the way to go. There is a great range of influence, from Emerson and Thoreau to Deleuze and Guattari. What unites these seemingly disparate sources, I think, is the notion that learning is essentially the construction of meaning and that art is the material constitution of freedom. For example, when you read through the many volumes of Thoreau's *Journals* what is so impressive is that he simply records what he observed and thought about during a usually aimless walk he took on any particular day. He doesn't take a walk—he allows his walk to take him—this is his pedagogy. He will more wander than walk. He'll observe the forms of cracks in the ice, and these cracks refer him to ideas about the world that have nothing to do with the cracks, and these ideas lead to the study of something else apparently unrelated. The universe of what his walk leads him to learn is ever-expanding, generous, free. This is learning as poetry—this idea of sauntering not only through the woods but through history, through knowledge, through possibility—finding yourself by carefully getting lost. And, of course, Emerson's essay on self-reliance is a manifesto for any artist, any citizen genuinely interested in democracy. I doubt if any of these texts have been read by the kids. But when it is their time to come to them, they will. **Angel:** I read one. "Self-Reliance." **Tim:** I can tell. **Nick:** I suspect that many of these texts might not appear as required—or even suggested—readings in most teacher-education courses. **Tim:** They're too

busy studying the stages of development. **Nick:** Let's move on to talking about your work itself. I'm particularly intrigued by the painting you recently completed based on Jules Verne's *From the Earth to the Moon*. In some ways it seems similar to and yet very different from your other work. Can you discuss what inspired it, where it came from, and the connections that it evokes for you? **Nelson:** Tim was moved by the title of the book, but he couldn't think of anything we could do with it. Then one day out of the blue he just came up to me and goes, "I think I have an idea. How about broken glass—glass glued on a dark canvas like stars?" And at first we all thought, "Oh, that's *too* corny." I didn't like the idea. But then Tim prepared a small canvas. He told me the problem would be to make the painting the color of the Bronx sky at night. So, as usual, we tried things on a small scale. And the first things were so close to the edge of corny that they were beautiful. **Angel:** They were so low-brow they became high-brow. They didn't work; they were so corny. I remember I came back from vacation and Tim and K.O.S. made a bunch of studies, and they were all really excited about the work. The first time I saw them I asked, "Tim, are you sure you want to do this?" **Tim:** The whole project was racked with doubt—and that's usually a sign that you're onto something important. The first studies looked like reject sets from *Star Trek*. They belonged in the Air and Space Museum. But two of the younger members, Christopher Hernandez and Jorge Abreu, became obsessed with *From the Earth to the Moon*. It was their belief and enthusiasm that kept the work going and growing. It was a long, slow process. I first got the idea one very cold winter's night. The sky was very dark, but clear, and the air was crisp. It was a full moon. The moonlight was beaming down on Barretto Street. The whole street is constantly covered with glass—sometimes I think that every night is *Kristallnacht* in the South Bronx. But in this instance, the moonlight was reflected on the scattered shards of glass, and the ground echoed the appearance of the stars in the sky. Dare I say it was beautiful? Careful, now, because when you see beauty in distress, when destruction or debris are aestheticized, this is a problem. But the moonlight on the glass *was* beautiful—and on Barretto Street you take beauty wherever you can get it! And I thought, "That's it. *From the Earth…to the Moon.* Boom!" The next day I sheepishly mentioned the idea to Nelson, then to the others. Chris got all excited and went down to the street to collect all the different kinds of glass. **Nelson:** Shattered glass from all over the neighborhood. **Tim:** After years of struggle, we finally had a connection. This is what starts the entire art-making and learning process. Then for another year-and-a-half you make studies, the techniques and the ideas evolve, and we finally arrive at something we all agree on doing. For instance, we agonized over what proportions the painting should be. But when we were in Washington, D.C. on a visit to the National Gallery we encountered our old friend Barnett Newman's *Stations of the Cross,* and we all looked at each other and knew that the sizes of those paintings were perfect. We wondered why, so we found Harold Rosenberg's monograph on Newman and checked the dimensions. We think the rectangle of the picture plane approximates the size of a crucified figure—and this strikes you intuitively. Then we concentrated on the chapter, "A Monster Meeting," from Jules Verne's book. This is the chapter where Audan, the adventurer, gives a speech declaring that "Distance does not exist!"—a proposition that the kids and I have spent hours discussing. And we spent a lot of time with Eames' classic *Powers of Ten* that has illustrations of the universe in its infinity. That became the connection—the cosmos and the sidewalk on Barretto Street. That moved me—that how the sidewalk outside our studio looks on a cold, moonlit night is also how the universe looks in its farthest reaches. **Nelson:** Taking those pieces of glass from the floor… **Tim:** City kids always call the ground the floor! **Nelson:** …and turning them into a work of art is like the title *From the Earth to the Moon.* From here to there. **Nick:** You've also worked through issues of proportion on a different scale. For example, the etchings related to Flaubert's *The Temptations of St. Anthony* at Crown Point Press. Compared to many of your other works, they're almost like miniatures—miniature worlds—very intimate, yet very physical at the same time. Can you comment on the process of working on such a small scale, especially after having worked for so long on your larger paintings? **Nelson:** First of all, it's difficult. [Laughter.] We didn't use any traditional drawing or painting instruments, like brushes. We were doing etchings on these really small copper plates. We decided to work on a small scale because we were just fooling around with the text, and the text is not whole. We made it small because if you take a piece of the text and you place it in a little space—three by two inches—you get a partial sense of what's going on. It became a little, violent world. We worked with acid, oils, salt…hair. **Tim:** The larger works are outer space, and the tiny works are inner space. But then again sometimes the scale—in terms of their effect on you—is greater in the little works. The large "Amerika" or "Animal Farm" works literally consume you. In the small works, you're drawn in. **Nick:** More than a few critics have seen in your work connections between the traditions of the beautiful and the imperatives of the political. Can you talk more about what that means to you? **Tim:** Sure. It comes from direct community experience combined with a sentiment I learned from Dostoyevski, "Only beauty can change things." I was recruited by the community to teach art in 1981. I came committed to the great traditions of twentieth century political art—Soviet Constructivism: Rodchenko, El Lissitsky, Stepanova, Popova, Tatlin, Eisenstein, and Vertov. I also was into the artists of the Weimar period, especially Heartfield, Höch, Grosz, and Brecht—the "blood-and-guts" school of political art. These are artists I admire and love—they make up the German expressionist political tradition. But when you look at some of the more extreme poles of this aesthetic—the war etchings of Otto Dix, for example—the strategy is to disgust. The idea is to show the horrific conditions of society in the hope that these revolting images will move people to become active in changing that society. But I think that towards the end of this century, especially with people constantly immersed in images of death from the mass media, people are used to images of horror, destruction, and depravation. Warhol shows us that even the stomach-turning image of a car accident becomes banal if repeated enough times. When I started working at I.S. 52 in the Bronx, the first paintings we made were predictably lurid in form and content. We made a diptych from the novels *Dracula* and *Frankenstein*—combinations of some very crude, cartoony, bloody, wild, and horrific images. Those first paintings looked like the fronts of the spook houses in Coney Island. A few days ago a curator I know told me that she saw one of the early works in a show in Philadelphia for the first time. She said that compared to our current work, those early paintings were "the real thing." But I think she was absolutely wrong, and she is mistaken in the way I was wrong when I first started working in the South Bronx. Because in retrospect I can now see what was going on: I was bringing my politically correct education and training in mainly European traditions of political art to bear on an area like the South Bronx. I was projecting my agenda on the community and the kids. Of course, there is really no other way to begin, but it got to the point where other teachers, the paraprofessionals, custodians, parents, and even the kids started protesting, "Tim, this isn't what we are all about." When that curator said that those first works were "real," what she was actually expressing is that the qualities of those early paintings—their crudeness, the brilliant colors, the surreal and negative and despairing imagery—corresponded with *her* notions—as an outsider—of what art produced in the South Bronx must look like. Once again the South Bronx is considered incapable of creating beauty. The community's fame comes from being a national pariah. The South Bronx is there to suffer—as visibly and dramatically as possible—for those who don't have to live here. The community was right, and I

Tim Rollins & K.O.S.

had to ask, "What do we do now?" I began thinking about those traditions where the political and the beautiful are successfully melded together. I immediately began reconsidering the beautiful wallpaper designs and working methods of the nineteenth-century workshops of William Morris in England. And, once again, the Constructivists' demand that radical politics be expressed in new, radical forms. But I also began thinking of American jazz and choral music—the spirit of improvisation and a less obvious, more enduring, and universal expression of injustice and hope. It became clear that our method of making the work was inherently political—that one could be vital and transformative but also elegant and beautiful. From this reconsideration, I think, came the "Amerika" paintings. **Nick:** To my knowledge, you have been working on the "Amerika" series since 1984 or 1985. What are some of the understandings that you have gained from such an extended engagement with a single, particular piece of work? **Nelson:** I feel, doing these horns, I am like the character Karl in the book. He really just wants to become an artist. Through the painting, I feel like I'm speaking out to the people who see the painting. And through the painting, I find that I do have choices in my life, and that I can change. I can do things about my life. **Tim:** "Amerika" has become the series that does not die. After the second one, I thought, "I'm sick of these damn things." I didn't want to continue the work. But when you get new kids, that's the first project they both want and are able to participate in. We have created this sort of open, democratic structure—like the scores of John Cage—where all the old rules are disposed of and anyone can

jump in and become an artist—just like the mission of the Nature Theatre of Oklahoma invented by Kafka. Anyone can make these things and that, I believe, is what make these works so engaging, energetic, and strange. Like its namesake, *Amerika* keeps demanding to be rejuvenated. In fact, there is now more pressure *not* to make any more golden-horn paintings, to close the series. Young artists are now pressured like fashion designers—people expect a new collection every single season. I admire artists like Richard Diebenkorn who made hundreds of "Ocean Park" paintings—these moving variations on a theme—not for market reasons but because he had the wisdom to know that it takes that long, that much play, to discover something new. **Nick:** As we were visiting two weeks ago, you told me that this was the tenth anniversary of your project, your work together. In some ways, it must seem like both a long period of time, and yet a short time too. What's your vision for the next ten years—individually, collectively? **Tim:** Three years from now, when I turn forty, I would like to celebrate my birthday in the new, completed South Bronx Academy of Art. I would also hope to see the slow improvement of our art work. Our work has become much like the South Bronx itself—a very two-steps-forward, one-step-backwards kind of development. I soon expect to have kids of my own, which will be interesting after my ten-year experience with K.O.S. And as the older members leave for college or other experiences, as new kids with different personalities come in, as I grow older, I realize I will not have the same relationship I had with, say, Rick, Angel, or Carlos. But that's okay. It's like a team, and it's the particular combination of team members that makes up the feel of the group as a whole. I want to see if we can take what we have done and create a school that will expand the influence of our educational success without giving up the artwork. It's simply not enough to impact the lives of only a dozen kids. If we have a fighting chance, we have the duty to make the project grow into a force that can have an effect on many others. We're going to create a school that will transform American education with great enthusiasm and hope.

(This conversation with Tim Rollins and Kids of Survival took place at the Hirshhorn Museum of Art in conjunction with the opening of their exhibition, "Tim Rollins + K.O.S.: Animal Farm," September 16, 1992. It is an edited version of the original one-hour-and-fifteen-minute session.)

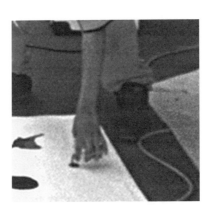

The Art and Knowledge Workshop, 841 Barretto Street, South Bronx

At the Art and Knowledge Workshop

April 23, 1993

FROM GRAND CENTRAL IN MID-MANHATTAN, THE NUMBER SIX train goes north under Lexington Avenue, then veers northeast at 125th into the Bronx. It is still early afternoon when I get off the Pelham Local at Longwood Avenue and walk one block toward Bruckner Boulevard—a wide four-lane that angles far beneath the vaulted Expressway named after it. Today is overcast, windswept, and cold, and after walking across the boulevard and under the Expressway, I enter an area of the city that to some, might seem like a no-place on account of its streets littered with trash and broken glass, places where drugs are used and sold, factory buildings that loom large and appear unattended, and gaping lots enclosed by cyclone fences topped with razor wire. As I walk up Barretto Street where the Art and Knowledge Workshop is located, a police car drives slowly by, its siren off, but patrol

Nelson Savinon arranging a preliminary composition for
the painting *The Scarlet Letter*

lights flashing.

I climb the three flights of industrial stairs in an old factory building, knock loudly on the double doors (as the sign recommends) and very shortly Tim opens the door, says hello, he's on the phone, come in.

I walk into the studio, which is an immense open space filled with work done, work in progress, and work just beginning to be imagined. Directly ahead of me is a large (incomplete) canvas from *The Red Badge of Courage* series; to its left is a large, partially wrapped *Black Alice*; to the immediate left of the studio entrance, the well-used library and study area; scattered on the floor are the wood segments of the *Pinocchio* sculpture; and in the distance, worktables, materials, and some large and small canvases from Hawthorne's *The Scarlet Letter*. Tim invites me into the office, where I take off my coat and sit down while he finishes his conversation. He's just returned from a panel session in which he and a number of others spent the morning discussing the design and development of an education program at Dia Center for the Arts.

After completing his phone conversation, Tim updates me about the developments that have occurred at the Workshop since we last spoke. His plan for an independent secondary school (the South Bronx Academy of Art) has been approved by the Board of Education and is on-line for opening in 1995. He mentions the group's being awarded a sizable commission for a mural project to be located at the Bronx Detention Center (he also discusses the byzantine politics associated with all public-art projects in New York now after the recriminations about the installation of Richard Serra's public sculpture, *Tilted Arc*) and that the mural will be based on the children's classic, *Charlotte's Web*. He mentions that the group is working on a new set of paintings from "The Scarlet Letter" series for an exhibition at the Rhona Hoffman Gallery in Chicago scheduled to open in May, and he talks about three new members who have recently joined K.O.S. The group, Tim also recounts, is still feeling the loss of Christopher Hernandez, a K.O.S. member and an eighth-grade honor student who was shot to death at home in a case of mistaken identity on Valentine's Day, two months earlier.

I mention that during my last visit, I found Christopher's ongoing work, paintings based on Jules Verne's *From the Earth to the Moon*, most moving. I recall how, for me, the painting seemed to break into multiple metaphors that cut any number of ways: the sharpness of the dream (and the struggle) to escape the force of earth's literal—and figurative—gravitational pull; the play of dramas that connected celestial, terrestial, and personal space; the contradictory ideas of transcendence and transformation, resistance and return. Tim mentions that this painting has since been purchased by the Hirshhorn Museum for their permanent collection.

The conversation then turns to current work. This afternoon, Tim explains, in addition to the group's activity on "The Scarlet Letter" paintings, several members will be continuing our study of Matisse and his work with color, exploring in visual terms, notions of freedom, independence, boundaries.

During our discussion, the members of K.O.S. arrive one by one, and after brief greetings and/or introductions, begin

Genuine collaboration

is a coming together of people to create something that would have been impossible to make alone. The simplest art partnerships join the work of two or more people together to form a single creation. A more elaborate structure for collaboration can be seen in the performing arts, where a group of individuals performs a work created by a dominant author or maestro. But isn't more than a combined effort required? A dialogue, a communication, a connection that transforms the participants can occur. Deep collaboration compels us to see ourselves through others. Truly collaborative works of art are commitments in time and space, cause and effect at once, even a form of love.

—Tim Rollins

to work. The members who show up this afternoon include Nelson (Rick) Savinon, a long-time member of K.O.S. and now a first-year student at the School of Visual Arts; Victor Llanos, an eleventh-grade high-school student; Jorge Abreu and Jamel Lewis (who proudly show their excellent report cards to Tim, who, in turn, responds to their accomplishments with similar pride and enthusiasm); and the three newest members, Hector Perez, Timothy Dargan, and Miguel Lorenzo. Later, Carlos Rivera (also a veteran member of K.O.S.) arrives and Tim takes him aside to discuss what I later learn is the status of his application to S.U.N.Y.-Purchase. This season, the group apparently does not include any girls, and I find their absence striking. I wonder about the reasons for such absence. Apart from Annette Rosado's participation several years ago, and despite what I have perceived as the very real, open, and sustained invitation to participate in the Workshop ("Everyone is welcome"), I'm uncertain as to the status of girls and young women in K.O.S. Tim has talked about how the Workshop bears resemblance to the artistic workshops of the Renaissance and its emphasis on the collaborative, graduated, incremental learning of a craft, but did these workshops, I am trying to recall, include girls or young women? I can't imagine they did.

I move around the studio alternately taking photographs and asking K.O.S. to explain or clarify certain aspects of the work in which they're engaged. Most of the activity centers around the paintings that will go to Chicago, since they will be shipped out next Thursday. Essentially, there will be four major pieces on canvas: one large work approximately five by fourteen feet, and three mid-size ones, each measuring what appears to be four by six feet. Also included will be a number of letter "A" studies on individual book pages.

As I walk around the studio, my eye is especially drawn to the almost completed mid-size painting to the immediate right of the unmarked large canvas. Its "A"'s are really passionate, sensual—sensationalized. I'm particularly fascinated by the large image of the "A" (done after a drawing by Victor) that dominates the right part of the canvas. It evokes a series of images and ideas that call to mind a Rorschach, or an explosion, or a union of two elements implying a powerful (explosive?) sexuality. This is an "A" of excess and extravagance, of visual and conceptual power. The more I look at it, the more I like the way Victor's "A" simultaneously suggests, and gives emblematic status to, the idea of love (Hester Prynne's—as well as our own?) as something supraordinary—a force that explodes the narrowness and smallness of the letter of the law that, throughout history, has sought to civilize and contain its energy. The other similarly sized "Scarlet Letter" painting isn't as moving. It's stronger in a compositional way, but it looks too studied, too carefully put together. The "A"'s are too immovable. But perhaps their very groundedness is precisely the point in this artwork, referring to the formality of her sentence: that this is Hester's place, your place. That this is you. In suggesting this kind of power, then, maybe the painting works as a kind of challenge to the viewer, saying, "No, you're wrong. That's not my location. That's your representation of it. I'm something completely different."

At one of the worktables, Rick is selecting from and con-

Tim Rollins and Victor Llanos working in the studio on *The Scarlet Letter*

Top: Nelson Savinon; Lower: Carlos Rivera

tinually rearranging a series of drawings agreed upon by K.O.S. for inclusion on a study sheet that will serve as a guide to compose the large "Scarlet Letter" painting. (Tim tells me that Rick is exceptional at this task, possessing a wonderfully intuitive sense of composition and placement). From time to time, I talk with Rick about the process he's going through, which he acknowledges is often very challenging since there are so many complex visual and conceptual associations to think about. At a later point, I return and find him reworking the compositional placement for a small, curving, almost brooding, enclosed drawing of an "A" by Hector. I find the image a provocative one and remark that its graphic qualities make me imagine it as a small stained-glass window. Rick then alternately observes how, to him, its shape seems that of a person's heart, which then makes me see Hector's "A" as an image of a heart's inner structure, as if displayed in cross-section for public scrutiny. Rick mentions that in these new paintings, the group was trying to develop images that didn't just look like "A"'s, but rather could be read several ways, like we were just doing with Hector's drawing.

At another worktable, Carlos works through a similar process for one of the small paintings for the Chicago show. At still another table, Timothy, Hector, and Miguel are busy "jamming," or working on their own penciled versions of the letter that Prynne is forced to wear. One of Timothy's interpretations looks like a blazing fire. ("Terrific," I think to myself. It suggests a multiplicity of psychologies: love's passion, intensity, warmth, unpredictability, destructive power.) Hector works on an image that, to my eye, takes the shape of a high, floating cloud (emblematic, perhaps, of love's lightness and fragility? its randomness and hypnotic power?) Miguel shows me a series of more literally derived letters—somewhat like formal letters from a typographical album, serif and sans serif. When Timothy, Hector, or Miguel think they've got a good letter, they show their efforts to one of the older members or to Tim, who approve their design or make suggestions for further development. Approved drawings generally find their way over to Carlos or Rick, who will try to incorporate them into the preliminary study for the painting, which the group will then evaluate together before starting work on the painting itself.

Toward the south end of the studio, Jamel and Jorge are mixing paint and pouring pigment free-form onto poster-size sheets of paper. They tell me that one of their objectives is to explore the creation of color in the sense of getting away from hues that look like primaries, a goal that I recall as key in Matisse's own work with paint and decoupage.

During these activities, Tim moves from group to group offering commentary that is approving, recommending, challenging. Now and then, he works on "The Scarlet Letter" paintings. He goes to the office to answer the phone. He returns and speaks to the entire group about the importance of reading on a daily basis if you want to be an artist. He reminds them that an artist is a person who knows things, who has and makes knowledge. He points out how one of the best ways to gain knowledge is by reading every day. He then invites everyone in the group to tell him what they are reading today—on their own and not as a school assignment.

"Jamming" on the letter "A": Hector Perez, Timothy Dargan, Miguel Lorenzo

Tim's doing all this, I surmise, to impress the younger members, mostly. To give them the idea that art isn't about just sitting around and drawing letters.

As this episode continues, Rick listens, but continues to work, engaged in his composition. Later, Tim tells me that Rick may have other things on his mind such as the presentation that both of them are scheduled to give at Yale University tomorrow morning. Still, no one escapes Rollins' questions about what books they're reading. Most of the members do offer some response, with Rollins occasionally pressing them to sharpen their thought by describing what their selections are about.

It is in this way that the afternoon goes by. Nearing six o'clock, everybody begins to clean up, and within fifteen minutes, we all leave together (the new members left a little earlier, having been picked up by their mothers). Out on Barretto Street, we say goodbye to Carlos, who walks west toward Garrison Avenue, and Tim and I, with Rick, Jamel, and Victor, walk toward Longwood. At the subway entrance, we say goodbye to Victor and take the train downtown. At this point in the day, our conversation jumps from topic to topic—from the continuation of an earlier discussion regarding George Steiner's recent book, *Real Presences*, to Steiner's astonishing erudition and reading activity (here Rollins ruefully submits that people don't have to read *anything* in this culture), to the craft of teaching (he suggests drama lessons for preservice teachers). On still a different subject, I raise the issue of style, asking if he and K.O.S. are moving to explore an artistic practice beyond the one that they've become iden-

tified with (limited by?)—transforming books into art. Rollins admits the complexities of change, mentioning that people want these kinds of works; they want to see what they already know. He mentions Roy Lichtenstein's witticism that you know you've found your own style when your work starts imitating it. He quotes Picasso's observation that "Style is death," and refers admiringly to Picasso's relentless working through a multiplicity of artistic stances. Embedded in all this is the irony, I speculate out loud, of working very diligently for years to develop a unique style in one's chosen craft, but perhaps not recognizing (until too late?) that this effort is also a powerful process of simultaneously constructing the terms of one's own confinement. Jamel, who has been sitting across from us and generally engaged in his own thoughts, gets out at 125th. As Tim and I continue to attempt to talk and listen to each other above the noise of the subway, Rick has his eyes closed, perhaps thinking of the presentation he and Rollins will be giving in New Haven tomorrow. At 42nd Street, the train lurches to a stop, and the door bangs open. I hurriedly say thank you and goodbye to Tim and Rick, shove to get out the door with everybody else making a change at Grand Central and within seconds, disappear into the overwhelming intensity and amnesia that is rush hour on Friday night in New York.

TIM: I've been thinking that art is like a student, a student for which most people have the lowest of expectations. **CARLOS:** I know what you're saying... **TIM:** Let's pretend that Carlos' name is Art. What if we assume because of who Art is and where Art comes from and because of what Art has done in the past, that Art is this and that and only capable of certain limited things. That's like taking this great potential, this possibility, locking it in a prison and throwing away the key. I love what we do with our project. We drive people crazy because they can't figure out what it is. Is it social work? Is it a school? Is it an art project? Is it a fraud? Is it socialism? Is it rehabilitation for juvenile deliquents?

NOTES

A portion of this chapter is based on "Kids of Survival: Experiments in the Study of Literature," which appeared in *English Journal*, September 1988.

References for the essay "Everyone is Welcome" are as follows:

1. Margot Hornblower, "South Bronx, 10 Years After Fame," *The Washington Post*, August 25, 1987, A8.
2. *Ibid.*, A1.
3. Tim Rollins, "Tim Rollins + K.O.S.," *Parkett*, no. 20, (1989), p. 36; Personal communication, August 28, 1992, New York.
4. *Ibid.*
5. *Ibid.*
6. *Ibid.*
7. Tim Rollins, "La Realización de 'Amerika'" ("The Making of 'Amerika'"), trans. N. M. Paley, *Figura*, (Autumn 1985), unpaged.
8. *Ibid.*
9. *Ibid.*
10. Michele Wallace, "Tim Rollins + K.O.S.: The 'Amerika' Series," in *Amerika: Tim Rollins + K.O.S.* (New York: Dia Art Foundation, 1989), pp. 46–47.
11. Tim Rollins, "Notes on Amerika I–XII," in *Amerika: Tim Rollins + K.O.S.*, p. 73.
12. Michael Brenson, "Art: 'Out of the Studio', Community Settings," *The New York Times*, February 6, 1987, C23.
13. Tim Rollins in Rosetta Brooks, "Tim Rollins + K.O.S.," *Artscribe*, (May 1987), p. 47.
14. Ron Jones, " Tim Rollins + K.O.S. at Jay Gorney Modern Art," *Flash Art* (March 1987), p. 107.
15. Roberta Smith, "Art: A Collaboration, Tim Rollins and K.O.S.," *The New York Times*, November 21, 1986, C28.
16. Barbara Kruger, wording taken from the poster for the March for Women's Lives (march for reproductive freedom) in Washington, D.C., April 9, 1989. Illustrated in David Deitcher, "Social Aesthetics," in *Democracy: A Project by Group Material*, ed. Brian Wallis (New York: Dia Art Foundation, 1990), p. 19.
17. Jean Fisher, "Tim Rollins + Kids of Survival," *Artforum*, (January 1987), p. 111.

References to the statements situated intertextually throughout the chapter are as follows (in order of appearance):

The statement by Octavio Paz is from *The Other Voice: Essays on Modern Poetry* (New York: Harcourt Brace Jovanovich, 1990), p. 151.

The conversation among Tim Rollins, George Garces, Richard Cruz, and Nelson Montes is excerpted from "Dialogue 5, April 19, 1989, 5:00 p.m., The Art and Knowledge Workshop Studio, 965 Longwood Avenue, South Bronx," in "Tim Rollins + K.O.S.," *Parkett*, no. 20, (1989), p. 62.

The statement by Annette Rosado is from Amei Wallach, "Survival Art, 101," *New York Newsday*, Part II, October 30, 1989, p. 16.

The statement "Devotion + Devour" was suggested by a memory of a painting of the same name (artist unknown).

The statement by Tim Rollins on genuine collaboration is from Tim Rollins, "Too Long Apart," a working copy of a manuscript provided to the author on April 23, 1993 about young people collaborating with artists to make photographs, p. 1.

The conversation between Tim Rollins and Carlos Rivera is excerpted from "Dialogue 5," p. 58.

"At the Art and Knowledge Workshop: April 23, 1993," is my reconstruction of an afternoon spent there.

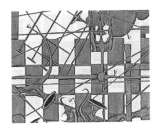

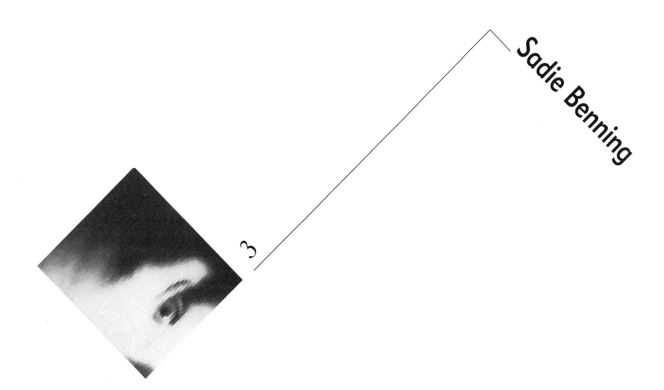

3 Sadie Benning

Permission?
I forgot all about it.

Trouble?
I got in a lot of that.

Sadie Benning *It Wasn't Love*, 1992

"That's Not How Life Is"

Sadie Benning began making videotapes when she was fifteen and was surprised to find "there was a community that would consider this valuable or art."[1]

She initially saw them as "just these secret experiments in my room."[2]

Before experimenting with the videotape format, she was in the habit of "methodically" documenting many of her personal experiences in the form of writings that she kept hidden in her room.[3]

She was born in Milwaukee, Wisconsin and grew up there.

Her family in Milwaukee included her mother, who was a massage therapist, and her mom's best friend, "a gay man who dressed like Dolly Parton."[4]

Many references to the city of Milwaukee seem invariably modified by the term "working-class."

Part of her growing up included coming to terms with the realization that she was gay.

She has great admiration for her mother. "I respect my mother immensely, and she accepted me. But that didn't make it any safer out in the world. It didn't make it any less scary outside."[5]

She didn't relate well to high school. "Everybody called each other 'fag' and 'queer,' and the teachers would joke about gay people. I just didn't want to be put through that abuse. I was in a really fragile stage, and I knew that if anybody knew I was gay, I would totally get tormented. School was really difficult. To be that age anyway is tough, but to be gay is just hell."[6]

(Consequently, she dropped out of high school just after her sixteenth birthday.)

Her mother and father were divorced before she was born.

Her father teaches at California Institute of the Arts, and is known in the art world for his experimental films.

The Fisher-Price Pixelvision video camera she uses to make all her videotapes was a Christmas present from him in 1988, but it's not like her first reaction was total gratitude. "I thought, 'This is a piece of [expletive]. It's black and white. It's for kids. He'd told me I was getting this big surprise. I was expecting a camcorder.'"[7]

Because the Pixelvision camera is just a "toy," designed for use by children, it's a cheap object, made of plastic.

"It looks like a space gun or something. There's no zoom or focus. It's really incredible—the focus is like the eye—automatic, with a huge depth of field."[8]

It works by transferring images onto an audio tape that fits inside the camera.

By regular "adult" video standards, its image looks rough-grained and unprofessional. Fisher-Price had taken it off the market, but recently I heard that because of all the notoriety the camera's getting now, they're really in a hurry to reissue it.

On New Year's Eve, after the Christmas when she got her video camera, she witnessed a drunk driver hit a friend of hers. On her way home later, she heard gunshots as she passed by a bar near her neighborhood. She recalls what happened then: "I ran down this alley. I ran two blocks to my house. I'm out of breath. I'm panicked. I had all these freaked-out feelings. I kind of wrote out scenes that had happened. I just set the camera down and it didn't judge me. It just listened. I used it to get things out that I couldn't tell anybody yet."[9]

After this experience and incorporating references to it, she made her first film, *A New Year*, a short video with in-camera edits, so it's just "one shot after the next, no editing at all."[10]

(Her first films are all edited this way. She says that her later films are put together differently, more deliberately. The first ones cost about $20 apiece to make.)

She worked alone in the beginning, transforming her bedroom into a film and production studio.

Most of the "action" in *A New Year* takes place within the confines of her bedroom (as do most of the scenes in her other films), because, as she's stated, "The world's not safe, my bedroom is. It's my space and all my things are mine, and there's no one there, passing judgment. Out in the world I see a lot of things and can be influenced."[11]

Her first films are four minutes long "because that's how long the tape is, that's all it took me to make them, not much planning."[12]

Jonathan Rosenbaum and Roberta Smith (two writers on contemporary art) have talked about the effect the Pixelvision camera has as it sets images into a rectangular black inner frame. They have independently stated that it positions the viewer as a spy or voyeur watching someone perform something very personal in private—like "a peep show" or "through a keyhole."[13]

Maybe because of this (simultaneous) pictorial compression and distancing in her images, the films often seem both emotionally intimate and non-committal.

(She communicates confidences about simple everyday events in deadpan voice-overs or in frequently misspelled written statements that seem only as simple as haiku is.)

She made two more films using her Pixelvision camera in 1989. *Living Inside* was done after she dropped out of high school and stayed at home for several consecutive weeks. *Me and Rubyfruit* emerged from her identifying with Molly Bolt, the young lesbian protagonist in Rita Mae Brown's novel, *Rubyfruit Jungle*.

Her family was supportive of her work, but she says "that doesn't mean that you don't get bombarded by the chaos outside— what you see on TV, what you see in magazines, all around you."[14]

Addressing the topic of her lesbian identity, she told the video critic Ellen Spiro, "When you're growing up, the media totally ignore gay and lesbian youth and gay people in general. When

I realized my feelings were nowhere on TV or anywhere else, I shoved them way down inside myself and tried to be something else. And then at a certain point, all those feelings surfaced back up, and I couldn't ignore them."[15]

Viewers have seen in *Me and Rubyfruit* an important step in Benning's work. They assert that it has more of a narrative quality, so it feels more cohesive, more structured than her earlier work.

This observation raises questions about the importance of "story" in people's lives and about satisfaction with how experience is framed. Or about what art's supposed to do with the "regular" world and its bombardment of images (media).

She says she only showed these first films "to friends" because she was unsure of what people might think of them. "If someone had said, 'Those are awful. Throw them out,' I probably wouldn't have done [videos] anymore."[16]

Then she brought them to California, where her father showed them in one of his film classes. A student was impressed enough by them to include them in a film festival he was organizing.

She's made five other films since that time: *Welcome To Normal, If Every Girl Had a Diary, Jollies, A Place Called Lovely,* and *It Wasn't Love*. Mindy Faber, the Associate Director of the Video Data

Bank in Chicago, the center that distributes her films, told me during one of my visits there in July, 1993 that Benning was about to release a new video, *Girl Power*, that she was currently working on (in Buffalo, New York.)

In 1991, the Museum of Modern Art featured her videos in retrospective. The Whitney Museum of American Art selected *It Wasn't Love* for exhibition in its 1993 Biennial. She was also awarded a Rockefeller Foundation grant ($35,000) in 1993.

(Her films have been seen at most of the major independent and experimental film festivals worldwide, including those in Berlin, Amsterdam, Toronto, Sydney, San Francisco, the Sundance Institute, and Washington D.C.)

Some writers have seen her work as directly related to the kind of contemporary artistic practice that deals with issues of identity politics, age, and gender in the social order.

An example of this is an essay by Lori Zippay which talks about how young video artists like Benning focus on "the poetics of the everyday"—or on scrutinizing the ordinary and commonplace in their home and life situations in order to make visible the ways that certain meanings and identities are made (or silenced, or erased) in a culture.[17]

I first screened her videotapes at the Video Data Bank in Chicago during several visits in July, 1992. Earlier, I'd heard about her work through the staff at Randolph Street Gallery, which is located on Milwaukee Avenue in Chicago. Randolph Street Gallery is an artists' advocacy collective/exhibition space that I'd been visiting on a regular basis since 1987.

During my initial screening, I watched each of her films several times in the Video Data Bank's viewing room. When the day was over, Ayanna Udongo, a video artist and the distribution manager at VDB, asked me what I thought. Without hesitating, I told her that I felt like I'd been "completely thrown into a totally different looking space."

I also told her that I really liked *If Every Girl Had a Diary*, especially the extended part toward the end where Benning films her hand so that it looks "practically human."

Finally, I also told her that I thought I liked the early films the best because "they were almost completely abstract, and you could imagine so many different connections to so many different realities in response to them."

During another visit to the Bank, I asked Mindy Faber if she'd be willing to forward a request for an interview to Benning, and she said yes, she would, but that I should put my request in a letter explaining the project I was working on (which I subsequently did).

She said that it might take some time to get a response because

Benning had been doing all these film festivals for the past two years and got really stressed out by the constant traveling and all the media attention and that she just wanted to get away from everything for a while.

"We didn't need Hollywood. We were Hollywood," Benning says somewhere near the very end of *It Wasn't Love*.

She has shifted her method of filming from the immediacy of the all-at-once approach to a longer-term process. "I shoot a lot of stuff all the time; I don't know where to put it, how it'll end up working. My last tape, *It Wasn't Love*, has stuff from two years ago—you may have noticed my hair was in all different lengths, different colors. How I work is I store up this library of images, then think up a story—this one has more than any other. Then I go look through all the stuff I have. I just made a five-minute tape that's about imagination, creating worlds in your head to help you survive, and young girls' desires—which are squashed in this world. I used images of animals, things that didn't necessarily have anything to do with what I was talking about, but suddenly there was this huge connection. My videos come together during the editing, not the writing."[18]

I recently read an essay by Jill Johnston that made me think of the autobiographical aspects in Benning's work. In this piece, Johnston wrote about the emergence of what she called a "plebeian autobiography" in contemporary literature—a form of writing practice where individuals articulate their identities (formerly excluded from cultural development and experience) "into existence, reconstituting their own histories...."[19] Johnston quoted a reviewer's response to one youthful writer's recent exploration of this kind of autobiography as writing practice. The reviewer: "Isn't it premature (if not presumptuous) for a young writer...to lapse into his anecdotage? Aren't memoirs, after all, the domain of elders...who are persuaded that a summing up is in order?"[20]

"I really want to fuck with narrative..." Benning stated not too long ago. "A climax and an ending is too simple; that's not how life is. I know that makes money because people are challenged in all these ways in everyday life; they don't want to pay to go be challenged. But I love experimental film, I love video. I don't like MTV, but it's an influence. Kids are growing up watching very artistic but also really shitty videos that damage the way you think. I like working with whatever you have, not waiting for something more prestigious, or to go through college. I don't believe in waiting for anything. I like the really raw stuff, things that are really cheap, very spontaneous. My work is honest because it's from just the raw materials; it's passionate. When you spend millions of dollars on this huge film, it feels so disconnected from any real feeling. There's a cold feeling to beautiful stylized texts or images."[21]

Questions: I wondered if it were possible that Johnston's idea of writing one's self into existence through the form of "plebeian autobiography" and Benning's work in the video medium could be unfolded across cultural domains to inform, perhaps, any of today's thinking/learning practice in school classrooms?

(Could we imagine children and young people engaged in what Johnston calls reversing the "notion of who has rights, whose voice can be heard, whose individuality is worthy…"?)[22]

Children?

(Imagine answers like *It Wasn't Love* as practice. Or *If Every Girl Had a Diary*. Had a Domain of Memoirs. Had a Lapse in Cultural Order.)

School?

"I want people to realize it's not just about 'gay youth,'" she's stated recently. "There's kids like me doing things in their bedrooms everywhere."[23]

She sees the "biggest strength" in her work as "that it exists," and thinks about "all the kids, queer or not, who sit at home, writin or whatever, that haven't gotten exposure, mostly because kids are taught to think that their creations are not valuable—'Watch TV. Worry about your appearance.' It's mostly a freak accident (and partly fate) that I am in the position I'm in today. Just three years ago I can see myself throwing my tapes in the garbage. I was embarrassed. So my tapes are honest because I never thought anyone would see them. I just tell the truth the way I live it, and that's what all this shit is about, life, art, being what you are, knowing what you like, and what you hate. So you can love, and create, and stand up for it, and you can hate, and stand up against it."[24]

A New Year

"A version of the 'teenage confession' with brutal and ugly
diary entries." (All images and video summaries courtesy
Video Data Bank.)

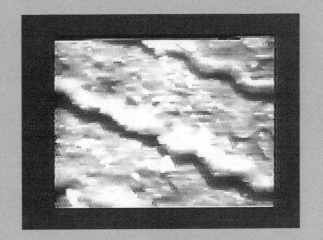

Living Inside

"When she was 16, Benning stopped going to high school for three weeks and stayed inside with her camera, her TV set, and a pile of dirty laundry. This tape mirrors her psyche during this time."

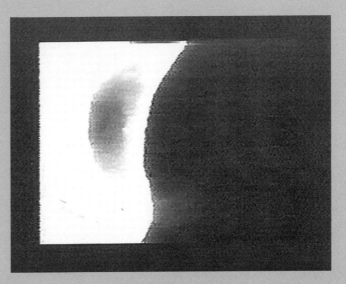

Me and Rubyfruit

"Based on the novel by Rita Mae Brown, this tape chronicles
the enchantment of teenage lesbian love."

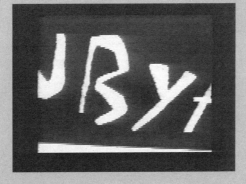

Jollies

"Benning recounts her earliest sexual encounters, tracing the development of her emerging lesbian identity."

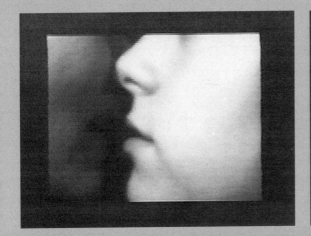

If Every Girl Had a Diary

"A young woman searches for identity and respect as a lesbian and as an adult."

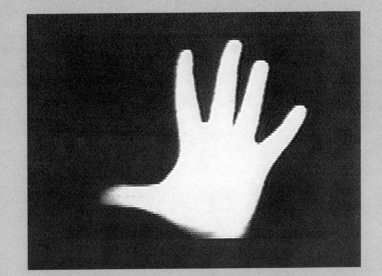
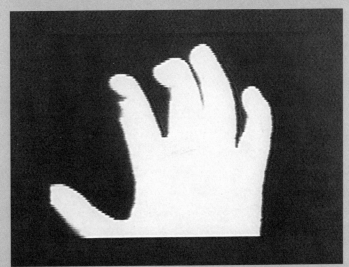

A Place Called Lovely

"'Nicky is seven. His parents are older and meaner.' *A Place Called Lovely* refers to many types of violence individuals find in life, from explicit beatings, accidents, and murders to the more insidious violence of lies, social expectations, and betrayed faith."

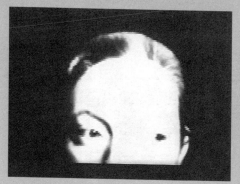

It Wasn't Love

"In Benning's most recent video she illustrates her encounter with a 'bad girl' through the gender posturing and genre interplay of Hollywood stereotypes: the rebel, the platinum blonde, the gangster, the 50s crooner, and the heavy lidded vamp. High-contrast Hollywood-cigarette poses, romantic slow dancing, and fast-action heavy-metal street shots propel the viewer through the story of the love affair. But Benning's video goes farther than romantic fantasy—describing the other facets of physical attraction including fear, violence, lust, guilt, and total excitement."

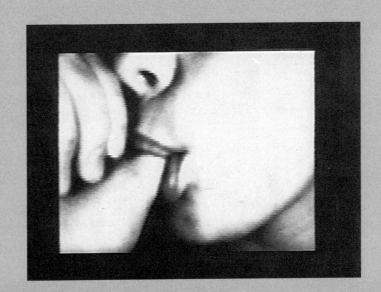

Statements

SADIE BENNING
Video Artist
19 Years Old

At a young age I questioned television because it had nothing to do with me or my family. I grew up in a single parent home with my mom and her best friend, a gay man. I was the butchest kid on the block. Television said we didn't exist, but it still had the power and influence to make me feel like a freak.

Of all the television I have soaked up in the past nineteen years, the most damaging and infuriating has been the nightly news, because for the majority of its viewers, it is reality. Night after night reports of women being mutilated, humiliated, raped, tortured, and kidnapped are followed by beer commercials. Both dehumanize us. Network news and shows like *America's Most Wanted* and *Unsolved Mysteries* sell women's pain, while mostly male television executives make money and enforce their dominance. Rape sells beer.

Television's images of brutality left me wondering when *I* would be victimized for being a girl, and for believing I was weaker. I have lived in fear of dark spaces, of walking alone, and of myself. Television taught me to feel that way. The news teaches women that they are defenseless against attack, and the United States government and courts tell us that when we do speak up to defend ourselves, we should know better. We are guilty for being women.

Are we, and will we be capable of imagining women to be something besides imbeciles, when TV represents us with no voice, no opinion, and parades us as slaves in front of our oppressors? Can we imagine change when the media controls our imaginations, when our hopes and dreams become limited by their restrictions?

When I started making videotapes three years ago, I didn't realize their importance. I had been taught all my life that because I was young, a woman, and queer, what I thought and felt was not valuable, and so I was embarrassed of my creations.

I wonder about all those secret superstars sitting alone in their bedrooms writing in their diaries, playing the guitar, and feeling half human because they're represented that way. Hoping a revolution will come along and change things. Not realizing that they *are* the revolution, and that their creations are the most powerful weapon in the fight because they represent themselves.

JOHN HANHARDT
Curator, Film and Video
Whitney Museum of American Art

Sadie Benning's Video Playground

> The toy is a materialization of the historicity contained in objects, extracting it by means of a particular manipulation.
>
> —Giorgio Agamden

Sadie Benning was given, at the age of fifteen, a Fisher-Price Pixelvision camera for Christmas. A toy camcorder for children, the Pixelvision camera records in black and white only, with half the resolution of standard video cameras. Benning manipulates the Pixelvision's imagemaking capacity by employing high-contrast lighting, using her hands and gestures to frame graphic full-screen compositions, and inserting hand-drawn titling. Further enhancing the video's graphic impact is the reduced size of the picture image, which is masked by a black border—the border of Benning's playground, a space to explore her personal history and coming of age as a lesbian. The oppositional images that she shoots and uses to subvert mainstream views of childhood and family life are shaped by in-camera edits that disrupt the action, and uneven sound reproduction that emphasizes the immediacy and "hands-on" feel of the recorded image. Sadie Benning has taken all of these factors to develop a unique style and refreshing form of narrative that expresses her real and imagined, visible and invisible, world of being a young lesbian.

The power of Benning's imagination is located in her struggle to break free of the closed space of her home and the routine of daily life, employing the camera as a means to break free of that domestic space and also break free from the technology of television. At the center of this struggle is a concept of play which extends from the camera to her active transformation of sexual roles and desires that she plays out in stories created for the narrative space of the framed moving image. The staged area of the Pixelvision frame becomes a place to play roles, cross-dress and mix genders and roles, lip synch a pop song, and place a scene from a Hollywood movie alongside a personal romance talked about and mimed in the studio of her bedroom. Benning's video becomes a ground on which to play out a desire for romance—the embrace of a sexuality freely expressed—a desire that pushes past the borders of

Sadie Benning

traditional television's narrative and its perfectly encoded middle-class melodramas and comedies.

Broadcast television—the channels of consumerism that flow out through the public landscape—has become the dominant media technology of the late twentieth century. The advances in technology and entrenchment of the codes of broadcasting have given us a privatized "public" medium that is a conduit for standardized entertainment. Benning's impact comes through her innovative and audacious break with this model of television. Television, as a slickly produced, homogenously composed ideology, proclaiming a heterosexual narrative—a norm of lifestyles and consumer culture that fits into and supports the commercial message of its sponsors, has created a world view of numbing norms that views children as desiring the ideals of the bourgeois family. Sadie Benning inverts these norms with a tough and playful imagery, imagery graphically flattened beneath the lens and the reduced frame of the screen. Benning's is a homemade video that loses nothing in its capitalized modesty; tapes such as *It Wasn't Love* (1992) are not made *for* the Pixelvision but because they *need* to be made. The voice of a personal and emerging lesbian identity is powerfully and urgently fashioned by Benning through images that directly address the medium—the camera as co-conspirator, and the viewer—as an intimate friend.

Sadie Benning's video has a driving momentum that is articulated through editing that fashions quick and smart stories, a mix of music and pop iconography transformed into a personal vision, a revision of heterosexist narrative, a poignant and vivid plea for a confessional poetics of self, an expression of desire, and a need to break the codes of technologically and ideologically determined television. Her Pixelvision has broken the apparatus of television, made it into a personal lens by which to refract and reflect her body and self, in the process offering a materialist re-envisioning of video as a medium of rebellion and affirmation.

It Wasn't Love

JANICE A. JIPSON
Professor, Educational Studies
Sonoma State University

Loose Associations: Seeing What is Ordinarily Obscured by the Familiar (A Response to the Work of Sadie Benning)

This was hard. Watching Sadie Benning and triggering on images of Emmie. Do other mothers watch this as if spying on their daughters? I felt trapped, uncentered, displaced. I felt like a voyeur. It reminded me of how I felt when I read *The House Tibet*.

Kids at war.

It was all oddly familiar, parts of me and parts of my kids, flipping me off to memories. Emmie is twenty. She wants the *Aladdin* video for Christmas. Last year she asked for *Beauty and the Beast*. She's serious and plans to collect all the Disneys, says her friends sit in the dorm and watch them on weekends. They know all the words to the songs. When she was in middle school I had to tape *Days of Our Lives* every day so she could watch it after school. I got hooked in to watching it, too. Now I just read the weekly summaries in the Saturday paper. Emmie has moved on to other things.

When Emmie went to the prom, she went shopping with all her friends and bought a low-cut black velvet dress with rhinestones. Her friends all bought black satin, and red tafetta, and velvet. They gathered at my house and got dressed in high heels, fixed each other's hair and all went to the prom together. No boys. When Jenny went to the prom we drove all the way to Seattle to buy the perfect pink frou-frou lace dress. My friend Gretchen fixed her hair. I was at AERA.

Jenny just finished college. She works full time for $7 an hour. After student loan bills she has very little left. I wish she could be silly again. I remember how I rushed at twenty-one into job, husband, kids. I wish I could be silly again, too.

I remember when I first realized I had to grow up. It was 1963 and I was a seventeen-year-old college freshman. A boy I was dating asked me if I had ever read Betty Friedan's *The Feminine Mystique*. I pretended and said, "Of course"... mentally adding the book to the growing list of things I had not read but now must...obligatory.

Watching Sadie Benning, I recalled something Maxine Greene said about singling out the "determinates in my life, the seductions as well as the controls."

Fiddling with the controller, I discover a new way of peeping in on Sadie Benning's life. Fast forward, stop, rewind, again, catch the beginning of each new scene… listen to the songs…"Blueberry Hill"…"My Funny Valentine." God, my dad used to sing those songs in the car.

I thought I stopped the video. A disembodied voice on the television sounds, "You made her stop crying." "Of course, I'm her mommy." I turn, catching a glimpse of a young girl clutching her doll to her chest. And even without knowing, I knew.

J. HOBERMAN
Critic, Film and Video
New York

Un Film de Fisher-Price

The daughter of avant-garde filmmaker James Benning…, Sadie [Benning] received a Pixelvision video camera as a Christmas present when she was fifteen. Her early tapes, like *Welcome to Normal* and *Jollies* (both 1990), were basically illustrated monologues that concerned the maker's sexual awakening in working-class Milwaukee. Most were shot in a bedroom overlooking a modest suburban street and were filled with teenage detritus. They were crude and blunt, but they allowed confessional self-indulgence to find its form.

Working on a nothing budget…, Benning created tapes that give literal meaning to the term "in your face." Peering into the lens in extreme close-up, she presents herself as a fragmented being of eyes and lips, developing a persona at once tough and vulnerable, provocative and mischievous, while punctuating her oblique utterances with hand-scrawled messages, bits of network TV, magazine cutouts, and bursts of popular music.

As critic Amy Taubin observed, Benning's early tapes were as much performance art as underground video. They were also heavily informed by a degree of personal necessity. In her junior year, Benning dropped out of high school and, with *Me and Rubyfruit* (inspired by Rita Mae

Jollies

Brown's novel *Rubyfruit Jungle*), *Living Inside*, and *If Every Girl Had a Diary*, came out as a lesbian—thus focusing the teenage angst that had been her previous material. Benning's latest tape, the twenty-minute *It Wasn't Love*, opens with the artist and another woman hugging and mugging in close-up while dancing to Billie Holiday. Changing her outfit nearly as often as she switches the music, Benning tells the story of a fantasy date that segues into a torrid version of *Thelma & Louise*: "Yesterday night, I drove to Hollywood with this chick...."

At nineteen, Benning has established a wide-ranging— if underground—reputation, having shown her work at the Museum of Modern Art, the New York International Festival of Lesbian and Gay Film, and the Rotterdam International Film Festival. The irony is that the format that provided Benning the means to articulate her personal situation (not to mention that of thousands of American teens), and enabled her to become the youngest artist ever included in the prestigious Whitney Biennial, no longer exists.

Yes, Benning still uses the same camera that her father gave her for Christmas back in 1988. But the PXL-2000 has been out of stock and unavailable for some three years. On the eve of Pixelvision's greatest success, Fisher-Price has taken it off the market.

LINDA MAURO
Professor, English Education
George Washington University

While I Hung Clean

1

At 15 I knew not
to smoke cigars
rob liquor stores
hang around bad people
or want to be alone.
I asked permission to suck my thumb.

Blood ran down the drain
while I hung clean clothes
to dry on the line.

My grandmother sang
America the Beautiful
on the front porch
and gave me Ken dolls
with large dicks
and an aversion to sushi.

I was certain of the world
I had become
a part of.

Sadie Benning

2

Yesterday night,
a midget in an apron, I
confused pierced noses
with shadowed breasts
on the trip to lovely
I never took.

Billie Holiday unwrapped
Hershey's kisses in an alley, and
I found freedom
in the back seat of a car.

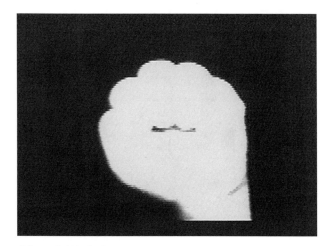

If Every Girl Had a Diary

CHRIS CHANG
Critic, Film and Video
New York

Up in Sadie's Room

The subject matter of the videos is Benning on Benning. To attempt such a thing at her age is no mean feat; Benning, in at least some forms of legal terminology, is not fully Benning yet. The videos, the first completed at age 16, are more accurately Benning becoming Benning—specifically, the becoming of a (homo)sexual being. Coming out in Milwaukee, she encounters the opposition. The status quo maintains a relatively seamless mechanism for the continuation of its program; the products of otherness are not available because the demand for them is not made visible. For Benning, an alternate route must be chosen: she comes out without leaving her room. The camera aimed directly at her own face, the background drops away into a pixel abyss. The shadowy indeterminate stage she sets herself within has the nondescript quality of dreamscape; only the main event is defined, the superfluous dissolves away. This creates a strong feeling of intimacy. The lens at times distorts her face in a fish-eye effect, offering the point of view similar to that of a lover's embrace. Her nose almost touches you, you can see the space beneath her eyes. As a closeup of a single eye fills the screen, we watch her open herself in a blend of bravery, trust, naiveté, and defiance. One never feels that this eye

Sadie Benning

staring back at us has anything to do with formal (self-reflective) notions of media art. It's just too frighteningly personal for that. Thinking of the Medusa-like tendrils of broadcast lines bringing this eye into strangers' living rooms, one begins to feel an almost overprotective jealousy…

Everything always manages to collapse back into the landscape of Benning's face. The dreams, memories, aspirations all return to her image, almost never beyond arm's length.

URSI REYNOLDS
Critic, Film and Video
Vancouver Island, British Columbia

I watched Sadie Benning's videotapes several times, and, to be perfectly honest, I considered turning off the VCR each time. I think it was mostly a motherly reaction. The intimate quality of a diary in living video offered more than I sometimes wanted to know.

I invited my daughter, Osha, to watch the tapes, and although we usually have a lot to say, that night was an exception. She asked me which part I liked best, and I said the part about being Hollywood, but not having to go there. She said she liked it all but especially when Sadie named and claimed her sexuality. She said that feeling powerful is part of being powerful. I listened carefully.

Osha carries a diary in her pack and exchanges sketches and poems with her friends. She invited me to reminisce over several old diaries she found in a trunk. I'm the first to admit that there are facets of her connections to youth culture that I find difficult to appreciate. I sometimes feel intrusive. Her journals, like Sadie's videos, describe the assertion of womanhood. On the one hand, the stories are tenderly held and boldly shared. On the other, as valuable as the telling of personal stories may be, they have at their core the lives of our own treasured daughters.

I do believe that Sadie's stories make the struggle to tell society's secrets less grim because they portray emergent agency and power. They invite a journey on the bold and open path. But while it is easy to imagine that going to Hollywood might be dangerous, I know for certain in my mother's heart that *being* Hollywood definitely is. And still they go and still they are, fearlessly bearing witness to their time.

Days later, I resolve to engage my contradictions. I want not only daughters to go and be, I want mothers, myself, to go with them. I will help guard the path with she-bear vigilance so that all of us may go and go and go. I will continue to listen.

It Wasn't Love

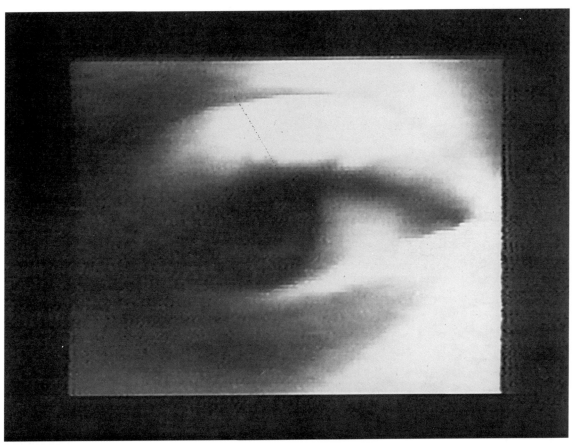

Living Inside

Sadie Benning

what childhood is for

fracturing the body in order to express

makes use of ordinary, everyday objects to deny the

or suggesting a connection between random events and evidence

using extremely close focus that magnifies the artificial

abrupt clips in

the manipulation of sequential time and cohesive

diaristic shorthand to get at issues of broader social

often takes form in brief, written statements that may or may not

exploring nonobjective means to be emotionally explicit

more of an abstract manner

the substitution of dolls

desire for a different

where individual expression provides the ground for scrutinizing

the allure of images and how they provide us with

does not always start from theory

responding to the necessity to make the familiar

exhibiting the self as screen and secret

divergent shifts that make evident tensions between

recording, performing, expanding, exchanging

individual awakening that reveals contradictions in cultural

story fragment

borrowing the incidental to establish the inferential

visual is not the same as

Video Responses

A NEW YEAR

1989

b/w video, four minutes

The last seconds of a TV commercial w/ Raisins dancing for Raisin Bran into clip of *Wheel of Fortune*. Quick panning over TV and *Wheel* set in bkgd. w/ contestants. *Wheel* game calls up multiple associations: circles, journeys, turnings, centered systems. Or a spinning. Or, Go ahead: Give it a try. What's to lose? Cut to clip of: a message (handwritten, difficult to read—a home-made graffiti? a ransom note? message in a bottle?): "I realized how crazy everyone is, and I realized what a small part I play in it." Stop video. Replay. Make copy. Repeat. This fits what. Pattern? Answer: Daily. Cut to image of Tabloids— in quick, jerky pans over words of today's world: "Grieve," "Predictions Through 1997." (over this rock music: "I shot the sheriff.") More messages: "A girl I know got hit by a drunk driver, her leg was broken and twisted like puddy." Mixed with images of toy car(s) to picture impact. Toy maximizes impact. Only toying? World pictured on/off horizontal. Even artificial worlds are shown as upside-down, degravitized when Benning? shakes up a paperweight in which The Holy Family is entombed in miniature snowscape. White Christmas never like this. Shake up. Cut to image of: playing cards flicked onto an accomodating surface from above. Aces tossed, buried, along with some hearts. Then many suits, face values. Quick assoc: Are images of Fate? Power? Boredom? No ending. Metaphoric drift. Cut to: A glimpse of an eye (an I?) for the splittest of seconds, Unblinking, observing, looking in/looking out. (A Spy?) Next message: "A friend of mine got raped by a black man," (then image: pouring Comet into sink, hand cleaning sink,) "Now she's a racist Nazi skinhead." (then image: Venetian window blinds pulled open and closed, opened and closed from an inside.) Sight…or Blinding? Just an experiment. More messages: Message: "Your easily trapped when you have an exscuse." Message: "My neighboor is selling crack as my neighbrohood dies, but our nation is addicted to a more powerful drug money." Cut to image of: Outside. Air. Sunlight. A dog running up from mid-dist. to close-focus. Jumps Up. Oops, camera.

LIVING INSIDE

1989

b/w video, four minutes

Like Second in a mystery series to read. Can read as secret and show. A game of hide/seek, open/close. Or as: A record of Facing up to it? But What it? A Voice that Seeks To Know(?) is heard at the beginning, asking: "What can I do?" Chorus of Answer Voices(?) form a series of responses, a list of matter-of-fact revelations, to end of tape. Chorus includes this Voice ("My mom watches Oprah 24 hours a day." "My dog is old and so is my grandma.") and there's a Voice of ("My dog likes dog food." "I know lots of people that like to eat ham." "I know a girl whose arm is made out of ham.") and there's a Voice of ("I should be at school." "Somehow I can't get myself to go." "It's so useless to me now." "I should be in study hall right now studying." "I haven't been to school in a week.") and a Voice that adds ("I hate school." "I only have one friend.") There's more. But is more—assertions or clues? Announcements or Evidence? Do episodes establish or resolve a mystery? Images are gorgeous, surreal: Facings and body parts pressed right to the lens make me think of a fictitious movie whose name might be—*The Journey to the Surface of the Skin*. An image of Lips (expansive as Man Ray's painting and sky; but also crunkled like Arnulf Rainer's photographic self-scourings). But mostly the images are Eyes looking, touring, pouring sight directly onto the lens of the video (an echo of Buñuel's *Un Chien…*"?—and that surrealism?). Optica. This often in scanning so slow, evokes thoughts of a Pan-optica. Gaze is thinking, unblinking, almost defying the vacant, recording mirror: Searching, scanning, peering, To find what? Image? Identity? Overexposed, a profile of face is now Alchemy, luminous against the dark: A ghost-spirit whose phosphorescent image glows/dissolves in brilliant, chaotic dark. Allusion: Facing the chaos? Or a twinning where the Picture is of Self and also of this deep unknown? Its own? Then ending in a slow-swallow, eat-dark sequence. The mystery of light-dark, the mirror and the me. The me and the eye/I—The living Insider.

ME AND RUBYFRUIT
1989
b/w video, six minutes

A shift from alchemy to story? Experiment to structure? Content: A Self focusing, (s)talking itself. Method: dialogue/or argument. Place: Inner and outer space + where mind/body Articulating lesbian identity through voiceovers and written messages skillfully/confidently staged. Not just argument between voices, but maybe more an Argue-Me? Extended example: "Who you gonna marry?" "I don't know yet." "Why don't you marry me? I'm not handsome but I'm pretty." "Girls can't get married." "Says who?" "It's a rule." "It's a dumb rule." Ex: "Look, if we want to get married we can get married; it doesn't matter what anyone says." Ex: "Good, we'll kiss like in the movies and then we'll be engaged." Out to touch in. Narrative inscribed within elastic visual imagination. Uses dolls, home, alone, focus. Record a "Fantasy" (label). Then images set to music, of photographs + lovemaking, pleasures pictured and imagined, like some lucky charms on key chains: Images as signals and symbols. Camera scans page with rows of photos of women's faces. Guess. Considering let's this Pleasure, but not around school. School is laws, authority, crazy. This bliss, not there. So Out elsewhere. (Kissing then, there's a picture of this wide open, unmarked sky with an audio of birds above air) Earlier, a sliver of a take: in a quick image-to-metaphor sequence, a box of matches (as in identities?), opened. One match removed, struck. Immediately (I'm me?) from whose tip an exuberant new flame bursts out—its own eye-like ruby: Yes.

IF EVERY GIRL HAD A DIARY
1990

b/w video, nine minutes

Images of self-articulation/surveillance? Starting w/long, slow, voiceless intro-pan across room from file cab. to lit lamp to SB's face to window. Cut to face in direct light and eyes/forehead/nose only: voiced statements that begin w/ tone abrupt, challenging, angry: "I was born here/ I'm not kidding you/ Don't look at me like that." Camera then explores dimensions of room ceiling, floors, darkened corners. Brief hold on SB's (?) cat looking up. As in: Hmmm. lives? how many ways to live them? Then to a floor on vertical from camera positioned in angled perspective. As in: what happens if I tilt the world I am? Then long empty spaces w/no monologue. In one an image of an empty sofa, inclined, hear a guitar played over. Projections: inclinations of what? suspense or relaxation? emptiness or just recording? Then, in a powerful, extended kind of "what's-eating-at-me" sequence, this voiceover while chewing up mouthfuls of food: ("It's only been a year ago that I crawled the walls/ And you know/ I've been waiting for the day to come/ when I could walk the streets/ people would look at me and say, 'That's a dyke.'/ And if they didn't like it/ they'd fall into the center of the earth and deal with themselves/ Maybe they'd return, but they'd respect me.") Images of feeding and nourishment of the body with recognitions and their articulations—but not just any recognitions; only those personally discovered, struggled with, gained. Moments later, camera pans to bedroom window (from mid-pt. distance) to outside. Camera as: a lookout? Or as: Look out!) Image includes window fan, half-open window, grillwork on balcony balustrade, and a grid of windows in brick apt. building across the street. A visual lattice that calls to mind a mix of layerings, maskings: concealing/revealing, bordering/ordering, enclosing/opening, barring/baring. Then in an extended clip, (app. 2 min.) of only imagine: Benning's left hand, sharply lit so it's almost luminous against a black bkgd., like a solo dancer on a stage of darkened air. Where hand (and during this episode a voiceover plays: "I want badly to yell out, but I don't want to cause a commotion/ Tension makes me nervous…") seems almost human. Then, as if it's struggling or awakening, I watch as it tentatively opens out, stands upright, measuring reach or resistance, crumples, falls to its feet, buckling its knees. Fisted, it coils tightly into itself as if with anger or boredom, slowly closing into a human stone (voiceover: "And me I'm numb/ I've got a headache/ I can imagine a million places I'd rather be.") Then an ending sequence, Benning's hand opening out in power to/toward what Imagine (?) Flash my own backtime: says Lascaux's wall. Says some new/ancient of days. Says connect to body shadows in paintings of Johns. Flash to video again: see on screen what could be a wave, then to clip of Benning's hand, palm spreading out, flipping in some atmosphere territory, sifting air. Then straightens up like waving again, or maybe gesturing stop. No. That's enough. End it. Don't look at me like that.

JOLLIES

1990

b/w video, eleven minutes

Visual/monolog chronol. sexual experiences from childhood through present, including straight/gay encounters. Benning as sexual autobiographer up in a somewhere room, visually cataloguing her sexual memories/awakenings/testings. Makes up own language, own vocabulary-content, own plug-in. Begins with positioning of two naked girl dolls in bed. Audio is Music: "I'm goin up, I'm goin down. I'm goin up and down and down and up...." No big star budget here. Locate a geog. of love from kindergarten ("They were twins, and I was a tomboy.") ("Like most poeple/ I had a crush/ It started in 1978/ when I was in kindergarten.") to adolescence ("So I got naked with this guy/ he was my boyfriend/ we were in a room full of birds . . .") to ("At 15/ I thought about her everyday/ and that meant love.") ("I turned 16 and I gave her my number/ and she gave me hers/ That night, I found I was queer as could be.") Mirror, mirror, turn around. I watch images otherwise. Struggle with, think: don't know. Look again: In head, flick video connect to Cindy Sherman's me/photography? Or Lorna Simpson's reverse/me images of identity's other side(s). Stop tape. Get *Shock Treatment*. Find: "Tonight let me remind you of July nights, of dancing fireflies, the sounds of crickets, a blanket of cool pine needles, slurpies, red ball jets and hot panting dogs. And as soon as we were eighteen, we got the hell out of there." (Karen Finley). Start video: Watch extended shave-and-dress sequence (Benning lathers and shaves face before camera, dresses in a dark shirt and light colored tie and waits for—). This a trying out and a transformation, a shedding and a redressing? Recognition on audio: ("But I'm not a man.") Benning's self-explorations shaved from most books of language development, human development, movie development, slurpie development, love development. Surprised (?).

A PLACE CALLED LOVELY

1991

b/w video, fourteen minutes

Production supported by a grant from Film in the Cities

Abrupt shift away from focus on issues of self-examination to looking outward broader persp. "A Place Called Lovely" as extended meditation (mediation?) on "A Place Called America." Evidence of crazy society that "scared her a lot." Benning's fear relates to media, political, social, personal representations of violence inflicted (from childhood-adulthood). Montages of images that burst w/ grace/conceptual power. Arranged in structured episodes. Opening image of houses across street w/ two police cars at scene. Followed by extreme close focus of child's mouth held open (alm. a dental shot) showing numerous missing teeth. Visual + voiceover ("Nicky Lugo was 7 and his parents were older and meaner.") reference to child abuse? Followed by a haunting sequence of men's long white undershirts and briefs hanging out to dry on a clothesline on hangers in empty backyard city. White, stiff, no body. Dance/hang like ghosts in wind. Or do they only seem to be human? Images simple, eerie, powerful. Stop video, see freeze shot: See absence, exposure. Image shivers, shatter object. Push play: Police sirens blare in the bkgd. Camera to long closing focus to the curving neck of hanger hook. Clotheswire on cold sky. Now see hook as image of instrument or noose. Flash to use in other practices, medical violence. Now image hook so close-up that it makes a question mark. Follow with sequences include cuts from home movies (?), a page from high-school class photo album w/Benning's photograph torn out. Stop tape, think (as if to suggest?: I can't/don't/won't ever be part of this because it doesn't recognize me to begin with); famous shower stabbing scene from *Psycho*; Benning flipping through *Starlet Detective* magazine, holding focus on ads for semi-automatic weapons, focus to words like "target," "battered bodies" then B. ripping *Starlet* mag. apart; a car crash she remembers from childhood; a game of chicken with knife stabbed between fingers of extended hand; a recollection of the twenty-nine children murdered in Atlanta in 1979. Voiceovers and written messages continuously refer to the randomness and pervasiveness of violence: "Tragedy, that can happen to anyone," and "Evil seemed common." Inspired closing episode where Benning targets mindless patriotism by photographing herself as a perfect constructed ideal. "Dolled up"(?) in blond wig and mayfair dress standing in front of a huge American flag that's hung w/stripes pointing straight downward. Representing herself as the culturally ideal representation of self: "Like one of those sweet little white girls/ who was some people's dream

of what was right in the world." As *America the Beautiful* plays in bkgd., Benning gushes with mega-beam patriotism. Then a very abrupt cut to a startled Benning waking up as if from a nightmare: ("That scared me too.") Ends with focus on tear rolling down cheek. Lonely and k(no)w.

IT WASN'T LOVE
1992
b/w video, twenty minutes

Watching, after others, see film shift. Away from direct focus/ social. Up tempo swayful/ playful. Long (one-and-a-half min.), opening sequence: studied, w/ title, credit, introduction shows Benning and her partner posing, prancing, embracing, dancing before camera to torchy music ("You go to my head") by Billie Holiday. Knowing borrowing/intercutting of music sets stage for romance (or: roam-ance? (or: roam-antics?) which then sharply manipulated/displaced by cut to music by Screaming Jay Hawkins(?), scream/singing. "I put a spell on you." (But who I on who you? Benning on companion? Companion as Benning herself? Video on Film Convention?) Traveling (by toy car in room) to Hollywood eventually with her tough ("F-u-c-k" penned in thick black ink on four fingers) double/companion ("She had an attitude") inspires(?) Benning to create a pose ("So I played it cool.") and the first of many identities. Costumed self as biker, then as wordly platinum blonde femme, then gets introduced (inter-deuced?) by double/companion to symbols in Bmoviedom/B-youth? (Spin on rebel takes: road journey/night escape, drugs/smoke, sex. Cuts on 50s rebel movies where boys/men?) But then a kind of cupid's call: "Suddenly I was in the mood for love," whereafter Benning recustomizes/targets other 50s identities from TV, music, and cinema: a 1950s rocker, a cartoon of girl writing in a diary, a hyper-emotional young daughter with parent (lover and mother?), and vamp eye(I)ing camera (viewer?) before making a lunge to camera to bite (sites of love's place in the 50s?). Then to voiceovers like: "I got nervous/ She got sexy." and (cutting on 50s cinema male tough/love talk where true love is equated with truest loss?) "She said/ Go ahead/ fall in love with me/ What else do you have to do?" Two extended sequences to video's end: In one, Benning as a gangster/outlaw with cane, cigar, leather jacket (voiceover: "She said, let's go to Detroit/ On the way we'll rob some liquor stores/ And when we get there/ we'll lay low.") Then, to voiceover: "We didn't make it to Detroit/ much less Hollywood/ Instead, we pulled into a fried chicken parking lot and made out." In the second, Benning, in a remarkable thumb-sucking sequence, fuses (or swallows) both identities using one hand to shape a sexual fantasy, an erotics of oral and body pleasure. Swallowing boundaries whole: as I/double, as child/adult, as male/female, as O/know, as now you think it/now you don't. With voiceover: "Yet in that parking lot/ I felt like I'd seen the whole world/ She had this way of making me feel like I was the goddam Nile River or something/ We didn't need Hollywood/ We were Hollywood." Then simple no end, with savvy distance: "It wasn't love/ but it was something."

It Wasn't Love

NOTES

Sadie Benning's statements at the beginning of this chapter, "Permission? I forgot all about it," and "Trouble? I got in a lot of that," are from her video, *It Wasn't Love*, 1992.

Quoted material appearing in the introductory essay, "That's Not How Life Is," is taken from the following sources:

1. Cherry Smyth, "Girls, Videos and Everything (after Sarah Schulman): The work of Sadie Benning," *Frieze*, (January/February 1993), p. 21.
2. *Ibid.*
3. Ellen Spiro, "Shooting Star: Teenage Video Maker Sadie Benning Attracts a Youthful Audience," *The Advocate*, (March 1991), p. 68.
4. Linda Yablonsky, "Profiles & Positions: Sadie Benning," *Bomb*, (Summer 1993), p. 18.
5. *Ibid.*, p. 20.
6. Spiro, p. 69.
7. Kim Masters, "Auteur of Adolescence: Sadie Benning, Talking to the Camera," *The Washington Post*, October 17, 1992, D7.
8. Smyth, p. 21.
9. Masters, p. D7.
10. Yablonsky, p. 18.
11. *Ibid.*
12. *Ibid.*
13. Jonathan Rosenbaum, "Girl With A Camera: Videos by Sadie Benning," *The Reader*, November 15, 1991, Section 1, p. 10. Roberta Smith, "A Video Artist Who Talks Through a Keyhole," *The New York Times*, March 28, 1993, Section 2, p. 33.
14. Yablonsky, p. 20.
15. Spiro, p. 68.
16. Masters, p. D7.
17. Lori Zippay, "Closer to Home: Personal Investigations of the Political Self," *Video Networks*, (August/September 1992), p. 18.
18. Elsie Harris, "Baby Butch Video: Elsie Harris Screens Enfant Terrible Sadie Benning," *Queer World*, (November 15, 1992), p. 33.
19. Jill Johnston, "Fictions of the Self in the Making," *The New York Times Book Review*, April 25, 1993, pp. 29, 33.
20. *Ibid.*, p. 29.
21. Harris, p. 63.
22. Johnston, p. 33.
23. Randy Gragg, "Close encounters on film: Candid intimacy sets apart stunning videos by teen Sadie Benning," *The Oregonian*, November 20, 1992, AE25.
24. Mark Ewert, "Sadie Benning" (Interview), *Mirage/Period[ical]* #4, eds. K. Killian and D. Bellamy, (August 1992), no page.

The form of the writing in this essay was inspired by the account of a visit that the artist Jack Pierson had with the painter Alex Katz which appeared in *Artforum* (February 1993), pp. 74–78.

References for material in the section **STATEMENTS**, are as follows:

Sadie Benning, "19 Years Old," *Visions*, (Fall 1992), p. 54.

John Hanhardt's "Sadie Benning's Video Playground" was an invited statement for this chapter.

Janice A. Jipson's "Loose Associations: Seeing What is Ordinarily Obscured by the Familiar" was an invited statement for this chapter.

J. Hoberman's statement is excerpted from "Un Film de Fisher-Price," *Premiere*, (April 1993), p. 47.

Linda Mauro's "While I Hung Clean" was an invited statement for this chapter.

Chris Chang's statement is excerpted from "Up in Sadie's Room," *Film Comment*, (March/April 1993), p. 8.

Ursi Reynolds' essay was an invited statement for this chapter.

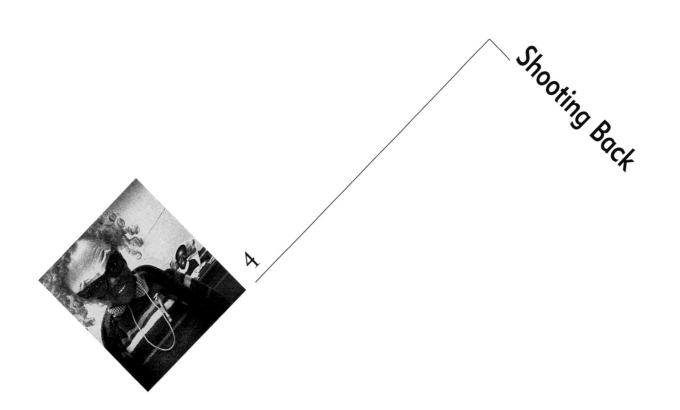

4

Shooting Back

When I come back home, I'm normal because I just go outside and play and do what I have to do. But when it's time to take pictures, I take pictures.

—Dion Johnson

Kid on a Street, 1989   Dion Johnson, 11

"Pictures of Their Own Struggle"

IN THE EARLY 1980S, JIM HUBBARD WAS A UPI STAFF PHOTOGRAPHER
assigned to cover the White House during the first term of the
Reagan Administration. An energetic and intense man,
Hubbard came to this assignment with a background that
included nearly two decades of work as a worldwide photojournalist with UPI and six years of graduate level work, earning a Master of Arts degree from Hamline University, where
he focused on Third World development, and a Master of
Divinity degree from Wesley Theological Seminary, where he
studied liberation theology. In his new assignment as a White
House photographer, Hubbard found himself encountering
repeated, official denials that homelessness was a problem in
contemporary America. Deeply insulted by "the insensitivi-
ty of [the Reagan] administration to the reality of people and
denying that there was a poverty problem in the country, a

homeless problem,"[1] Hubbard began documenting the homeless in the Washington, D.C. area, where poverty and homelessness are a particularly compelling reality for thousands of individuals, many of whom are children. Motivated in part by the idea of ministry as a force to translate the gospel message into social action and by the power of the photographic medium to convey a powerful message, Hubbard recorded the homeless on the streets, in parks, and in community shelters, sometimes working with the late Mitch Snyder, an activist for the homeless that city. These efforts culminated in a nomination for a Pulitzer Prize in 1986, and, in 1991, the publication of the book *American Refugees*, a photographic account of people who "are our neighbors…forced into exile by catastrophic circumstances that are beyond their control, but [whose] separation from the predominant culture is as total as if they had been deported to another land."[2]

It was also during this time that Hubbard made the decision to leave his position at UPI and consider teaching photography to the homeless children he encountered in the shelters he visited. The idea for this decision was generated when Vanessa Johnson, a homeless mother living at the Capitol City Inn (the largest homeless shelter in the District at the time) showed Hubbard some pictures her son, Dion, had been taking with her instamatic camera. Dion's interest in the photographic medium impressed Hubbard: "I was touched by his pride in the pictures. I wanted to spend some time with him working on his photography. I thought it would be a way for me to give something back. There were seven hundred other kids living there, and everytime I'd be with Dion, the

other kids would come up and ask if they could take pictures."[3] Recognizing the power of this interest and its connective potential with his own set of advocacy concerns, Hubbard developed the idea to have sheltered children in Washington, D.C. photograph their own world by giving them a camera "to take pictures of their own struggle"[4] with poverty, prejudice, and an uncaring government, and then to display their work in a major exhibition.

In early 1989, Hubbard approached Philip Brookman, Director of Programs at Washington Project for the Arts, a socially progressive, community-oriented metropolitan art organization/exhibition space in downtown Washington with the idea for his educational/artistic/cultural project. Soon afterward, as Brookman has noted, "Our collaboration began at the Community of Hope Shelter, where an answering machine, giggling with kids' voices, named the project Shooting Back."[5]

Guided by Hubbard and other professional photographers who volunteered their expertise, children at Community of Hope learned about the technical aspects of photography in a series of weekly workshops held at the shelter. There was only one rule that Hubbard established for children to follow: "Shoot within one block of the shelter; document that one block of reality."[6] Within several months, the workshops were expanded to include a broader range of activities and sites. Soon, Shooting Back became The Shooting Back Education and Media Center—a non-profit organization through which a growing number of professional and amateur photographers volunteered to teach weekly after-school workshops at six other shelters in the metropolitan area. In March 1990, an actual facility for The Shooting Back Education and Media Center was established, complete with darkroom capabilities and a modest work and meeting space. Taking advantage of this permanent location, Shooting Back offered an initial six-week Summer Program in photography, media, and interarts beginning in June. During this program, children worked with staff and professional photographers and writers, who assisted them with developing their expressive talents in the image and print media. As Shooting Back's programs developed in these locations, there was an active response from many parts of Washington's professional, corporate, social, and artistic communities: "Some [people] taught photography in the workshops organized by the newly established Shooting Back Education and Media Center. Some raised financial support, and others brought new and innovative ideas to the table."[7] Still others provided access to media resources, photographic equipment and film supplies. In September 1990, this eighteen-month series of collaborative efforts uniting the talents of individuals and groups representing multiple cultural interests and experiences, culminated in a major photographic exhibition, "Shooting Back: Photography By and About the Homeless," at the Washington Project for the Arts, in which the work of fifty-three homeless children and teenagers was displayed.

The diversity of photographs and level of artistry displayed at this exhibition immediately placed Shooting Back in the larger public eye. The photographs taken by the young boy and girl photographers showed children enjoying themselves at play, either alone or with their friends; they showed children affirming and creating their identities by posing for the camera with directness and grace; they showed images of families taking pleasure in the simple moments of daily life and in each other's company; they showed what the nation's capital looked like from their own viewpoints and from where they lived; and they pictured these fleeting enjoyments and recognitions against the chaos and the horror of shelter life where privacy and safety, protection and survival are not guaranteed on a daily basis. While much of the jolting power of this exhibition came from the juxtaposition of images that subverted cultural and media depictions that all too frequently represent the urban homeless as lacking in hope and promise, it also came from the subtle and often unexpected ways the photographs forced viewers to confront parallel issues of stereotypic attitudes and behavior, the tremendous—almost surreal—disproportion of wealth in the nation's capital, the vacancy of governmental promises during the 1980s about human rights, and questions of what should be done now.[8] Since its original showing in Washington, the "Shooting Back" display has gone on a national tour organized by the Denver Children's Museum.

After the exhibition in the nation's capital, Shooting Back's focus was broadened to include the teaching of photographic and writing skills to non-homeless children and young people living in Washington. This repositioning included additional staff and volunteers working with children in projects lasting 3–15 weeks throughout the year in various non-shelter community locations across Washington. Under the directorship of program coordinator Marie Moll, children and Shooting Back staff worked after school and on Saturday afternoons at these locations and at Center headquarters itself, where instruction in photography was often linked to other arts-related, personal enrichment activities such as writing, media, and book production.

In 1991, Hubbard expanded Shooting Back to include a second Education and Media Center in Minneapolis, Minnesota, which has been continuously directed by Wes Brown. This extended effort—coordinated with the newly established Native American Youth Project—was designed "to bring photography and writing workshops to Indian youth nationwide to document American Indian life through the eyes of young people."[9] An initial phase of this program began in July of that year with weekly workshops for urban Native American youth; a second, "outreach" phase saw Hubbard, Moll and Brown, taking their photographic equipment and mobile darkroom to conduct additional workshops with Native American children on reservations in the Central Plains and Southwest.[10]

One of the more extensive projects taken up by Shooting Back-Washington took place during the summer of 1992 when program staff collaborated with personnel at the Smithsonian Institution's Experimental Gallery and with seventy-five community youth and adults to produce "Community Bridge," the photographic component of the larger exhibition, "Kid's Bridge." Developed by the Children's Museum of Boston, "Kid's Bridge" was designed as a multi-faceted, participatory, hands-on experience providing the opportunity for children and adults to develop a deeper awareness of issues related to identity, ethnicity, and racism in contemporary America, and the opportunity for children to define and develop their articulations of these issues from their own perspective.[11] In preparation for the photographic component of the exhibition, Shooting Back staff, interns, and volunteers conducted a series of weekly photography workshops with Washington, D.C. youth at seven community centers/organizations. During these workshops, children learned basic photographic skills, and developing, processing, and mounting techniques. Young people were then invited to document "people and places in their neighborhoods, [record] daily events of importance to them, and [explore] museums, parks and city gardens on photo field trips."[12] Children also provided written statements accompanying their work describing their relation to the project in their own voices and from their own experience. The children were also actively involved in planning the show itself, something the original group of young photographers did not do with the WPA exhibition. Their work was initially displayed at the Smithsonian Institution's Experimental Gallery in October and November, 1992, and, through the Smithsonian Institution's Traveling Exhibition Service (SITES), will be exhibited at selected locations nationwide through 1996.[13]

In 1992, three of the children (Dion Johnson, Charlene Williams, and Daniel Hall) whose work featured prominently in the original WPA Shooting Back exhibition began their own for-profit photography project, called "Dion and Friends." Under the direction of Ella McCall-Haygan, a former chief social worker at the Capitol City Inn who orginally helped Hubbard promote the idea of children at the shelter becoming active with photography, "Dion and Friends" have used their experience at Shooting Back as a base from which to independently explore and exhibit new possibilities for artistic expression and social commentary. During the past two years, the group has been invited to do photographic work for the National Urban League, The Children's Defense Fund, The Black Caucus, and for the inaugural celebration of President Clinton in January 1993. An exhibition of their work for some of these organizations was recently displayed in the show, "Young Visions: A Look at Our World Beyond Homelessness," at the Experimental Gallery from September 1992 through March 1993. Currently, the group is working two afternoons a week after school at the Corcoran Museum of Art creating a video that speaks to issues of substance abuse.

The various Shooting Back exhibitions, programs, related collaborations and independent projects have generated extensive institutional exposure and attention. Articles generous with praise for Hubbard, his co-workers, and the Shooting Back photographers have appeared in such varied media sources as *The New York Times*, *The Washington Post*, *Life*, and *Museum and Arts*. A list of institutional support for Shooting Back is similarly impressive. In 1992–93 alone, for example, nineteen national and international foundations committed funding support for program activities, workshops, and ongoing evaluation. And in the spring of 1993, the Shooting Back Gallery, displaying photographs taken by children in the program's various projects, was opened in one of downtown Washington D.C.'s more prominent corporate locations, five blocks from the White House.

In the midst of its fourth year of operation, Shooting Back and its various projects continue to evolve in the flux of a complex social/cultural/educational/artistic field. What was a singular idea only several years ago, is now a multi-sited enterprise struggling with the actualities of its own industrialization: rapid development, program promotion, continuous reorganization, and ongoing project evaluation, as well as with the reality of retaining the clarity of its original vision: the necessity of making the familiar appear real. Like a series of photographs slowly developing, Shooting Back is open to name. Its identity is shifting and variable, simultaneously disclosing and transforming the pictures of its own image.

You know, it's just a picture. Not the real thing.

—Daniel Hall

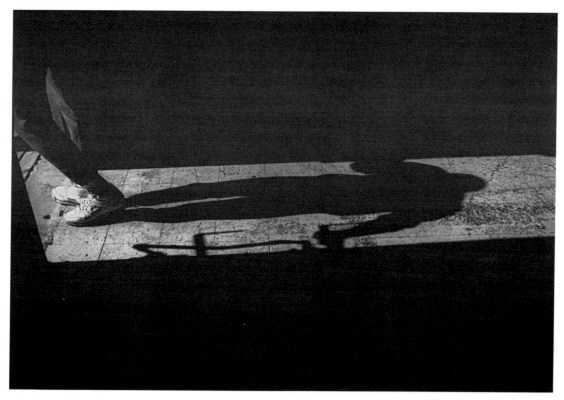

Shadow, 1990   Norman Heflin, 8

Fire Escape, 1989   Calvin Stewart, 17;   *Malcolm X Park*, 1989   Daniel Hall, 9

Girl at Back Door, 1990   Norman Heflin, 8;   *Property*, 1989   Calvin Stewart, 17

Conversation with Savon MacLemore (age 10), Sabrina Greeley (10), Tameka Atkinson (9), and Michael Sesay (14).

Nick Paley: How did you get involved in working with Shooting Back, and how long have you been taking photographs? **Savon MacLemore:** Mrs. Barron [Cynthia Barron is the After School Program Director at New Community Center. Barron and Marie Moll established Shooting Back as a community site at New Community in summer 1992] and the staff were saying we're going to be doing cameras, checking cameras and stuff out with Shooting Back like about next week, and this was a couple of months ago, before we started coming to Shooting Back. So that's really how I got started. **Tameka Atkinson:** Just since last summer. **Michael Sesay:** I've been working for a couple of months. I just came here to the After School Program, and Mrs. Barron told me about Shooting Back. She asked me if I wanted to join them, and I said yes. **Nick:** What have you all been taking pictures of? **Michael:** I took pictures of trees, houses, and dogs. People. I take pictures of everything I see. **Tameka:** Dogs, the cat. Me. I take pictures of my sister—and me and her [Sabrina]. **Sabrina Greeley:** I like taking pictures of us [Tameka and herself] together. **Savon:** I take pictures of a lot of things. I photographed dogs, rocks. I photographed trees, a church, my old school, Cleveland Elementary. I photographed a store, myself, some of my friends, birds. **Nick:** Do you think your photographs are any good, Savon? **Savon:** Yes. Some of them. Some of them are bad because I didn't use the needle that's supposed to be straight when you take a picture. **Nick:** How

can you tell when your photograph is good? How does your eye, your mind tell you that? **Savon:** Because *I* took the pictures—nobody else took them. *I* took them. So that means to tell me that *I* did a good job at doing what I did. **Nick:** But let's say you've taken a lot of photographs, and you're going through the contact sheets. How do you pick the ones that are *really* good? **Savon:** They have to be showing out real good. So say if you have a picture, and it was kind of faded. That wouldn't be a *good* picture, because if you tried to blow it up and you put it in the thing [enlarger] to see if it was good and then you put it in the liquids—the opener, the stopper, and all that stuff—and it wouldn't come out because it was a bad picture. You need a *clear* picture that you can *see*. You don't need a picture you can hardly see. If you can't hardly see the picture, it's not good. **Nick:** What's the easiest part about taking pictures? **Tameka:** All you have to do is snap. But you have to focus on what you're going to take. Sometimes it's hard, and sometimes it's easy. Depends on where you're at. Like if you were here, you would take mainly pictures of plants, trees, gardens. **Savon:** The easiest part is you get to take a picture of anything you want. That's the easy part— and you don't have to be telling what you take a picture of and you can just show the reaction of how you're taking it and the way, like, the motions that you take it—upside down, sideways, diagonal. **Michael:** You can just look at things and snap them. **Nick:** What's the hardest part? **Savon:** Putting the needle straight. The needle is for the picture to be straight, not crooked. And you want your picture to be straight, or your picture won't come out. **Michael:** Fixing the film inside, like when you're trying to put the film inside the camera. And printing. That's hard, too—to try and take out the film inside the roll and put it back, because you can't see anything inside a darkroom. **Nick:** If you had a chance with one photograph that you took to say something to the people of Washington, or to the President, what would you say in your photograph? What would it look like? **Tameka:** To make a point? **Nick:** Yes, *your* point. **Tameka:** I would take a picture of Shaw [the neighborhood] and my school because today somebody got shot in front of my school, and we were getting into a van and the person fell to the ground. Everybody screamed. *Every*body was so loud. And we ducked and Mrs. [unintelligible] said, "Duck! Duck! Duck!" and she just drove away like this [here Tameka hunches over in her chair]. I would like to make a point that I don't like the violence. That the surroundings are too dangerous. **Sabrina:** Of all my friends. 'Cause my friend's brother—he got shot in the head. 'Cause we were there one night, I went over to my friend's house. And she was telling me that her brother was around the corner, so we say we won't go around. We heard gunshots, and the next thing we went around there, and her brother was dead. And she started screaming. And I didn't know what happened. It was a shootout, and this man came up and all my friends said, "Do you know anything about how he got shot? Was he involved with any kind of drugs?" He was saying that he did do kind of a little bit of drugs, and then the lady, his mother, said that he

was doing it for his friends cause his friends threatened to kill him. He had the money in his pocket, and I guess that's why he got shot. **Nick:** What would the title of your photograph be? **Sabrina:** I would title it, "See a difference." **Savon:** I'd take a picture of people dealing drugs. And I'd say to the President and tell him that "*This* is why were losing our people." **Nick:** Can you tell me what you'd specifically have in your picture? **Savon:** Yes. Have the people who are just giving it to them. Just giving them the drugs, and they handing them the money, and they giving them the drugs. **Nick:** Have any people—photographers, people, artists—influenced you in your taking pictures? **Savon:** I like artists, because I'm gonna be an artist when I grow up. I like Michelangelo. **Nick:** Why Michelangelo? **Savon:** He's a great painter. **Nick:** And how does he inspire you? **Savon:** Well, just hearing about his paintings, his pictures, the way he did them. Being an artist, it's fun. I mean, my friends think I can draw very, very good. And I know I can draw *very* good. So it just makes me feel good to know. **Nick:** Does photography help you in school at all? **Savon:** It's different. But I can tell you a way it helps. By picturing stuff, you have to *remember*. You have to *remember* how to take the picture. You have to remember to put the needle in the right place. Like in your school you have to remember what's 1 + 1, or what's 2 + 2. So it's *remembering*. **Sabrina:** It's boring at school, and it's fun here. You get to take pictures of your own self and other people, and at school you just do a lot of work. **Nick:** What are you going to go out and shoot today? **Michael:** I'll probably take a picture of a church—and if I can find a tree in front of it, a dry tree, not with leaves on it. **Savon:** I don't know if they're going to take us out and shoot or not. If they do, I'll take some pictures of animals or people—and me. Take a lot of pictures of me, mostly.

(This conversation is an edited version of a discussion held at Shooting Back-New Community Center, April 14, 1993.)

Girls, 1989   Dion Johnson, 11

Boy in Shelter, 1989   Tamicka Hodge, 12

Shooting with Kirsten, Angie, and William

This afternoon I join Kirsten Neves, a Shooting Back intern, and two students, Angie Campbell and William Cawthorne, for a shoot. Home base for today's photography session is the New Community Center, a community action/educational organization serving the residents of the Shaw neighborhood in Washington, D.C. The New Community Center is one of Shooting Back's several community-based sites in the nation's capital and today Rachel Clark (Shooting Back-Washington's new co-director with Doug Sanford, appointed to replace the departing Marie Moll) and Kirsten have divided a small group of students into two mini-groups: Rachel takes Sabrina Greeley, Savon MacLemore, Tameka Atkinson, and Michael Sesay back to Shooting Back's Education and Media Center on 18th Street, where they will be learning darkroom and printing techniques, and Kirsten will be working with the remaining students on a shooting session.

It's a bright, warm, mid-April afternoon, and a number of students haven't shown up. Poised and apparently experienced with such comings and goings in attendance, Kirsten takes them in stride and doesn't miss a beat in telling the students what the plans are for the afternoon. Kirsten has been working with Shooting Back as an intern since January, as part of a field program arranged through her school, Marlboro College in Vermont, where she is pursuing studies in urban education. As for the students, Angie is ten, and a Shooting Back veteran, having taken part in the program since last summer. She's bright and vivacious, and today she's dressed in an oversized day-glo windbreaker whose hue, it seems to me, perfectly matches her spirit and zest for action. William is also ten but seems more interested in being ill-tempered to Angie today for a reason I can't understand. For her part, Angie responds by giving absolutely no indication of hearing, much less seeing, William even though the two of them are standing no more than two feet apart. Another student, Sam, who is eight, is also scheduled to go with us. When I go to find him, he is hiding under a desk in New Community's front hallway, playing hide-and-seek with several friends; when I tell him that we're leaving soon and would appreciate his joining the group, he tells me that he has decided to opt for staying where he is rather than coming with us on our shoot.

Kirsten has already helped Angie and William load film into their "point-and-shoot" cameras, and she gives the children final instructions about how their session today is connected to a larger project that they're going to be working on in the final weeks of the semester. As we leave New Community and walk west on S Street, Kirsten tells me that there are five weeks left in the spring program, and they've still a great deal of work to do. Kirsten has planned for her group to produce a book about their community, the Shaw neighborhood, documenting their work with photographs they take and print, supplemented with written commentary. Kirsten tells me that she really wants to see this project accomplished; however, she also makes it clear that while completing the book is important to her, it's also crucial for the children to have something concrete that affirms their

No title, 1993   William Cawthorne, 10

work together this semester. Not altogether sympathetic to Kirsten's worthy objectives, Angie and William appear interested in other things besides photography today. William has started up his teasing and challenging again, and Kirsten and I decide to split our small troupe up, with me taking William down 8th Street and Angie going with Kirsten heading west on S. Shouting above the traffic, we agree to meet back at New Community in an hour, around 5:30.

For nearly a block William and I walk in silence. I am partially taken aback by his confrontations with Angie and partially waiting to see what he would say first. William may have his own reasons for not venturing anything, especially since we've just met. (Be aware; be careful. Keep a straight edge up?) But my approach gets us nowhere, so I ask William what he likes to take pictures of, whether he has any brothers or sisters, how long he's been working in Shooting Back. Silence. All of a sudden, we're walking down a block I don't recognize, and I realize that I'm in a world I don't know on a daily basis. I feel as if my idea of role identity is being abruptly reversed. Who's taking whom on a shoot? Where? William cuts into a parking lot bordered by recently constructed high-rise housing that absorbs the warm afternoon light. At the far end of the parking lot, I notice a scuffle in progress—not too serious, I immediately conclude, but who knows? And what's *not* serious in this city already jittery by a springtime of random violence, drive-by shootings, and a near-record homicide rate? I feel myself getting too wound up in these projections (then I feel myself asking why I'm feeling this) and shout up to William, now a good ten feet ahead of me,

No title, 1993 William Cawthorne, 10

"Hey, William, where are you going?"

"You're asking too many questions."

Not immediately, but soon enough after his reply that I took it as a subtle kind of understanding on William's part, an offer:

"I'm going to the playground. You coming?"

"What playground?"

I follow William down a long sidewalk that angles into an opening (surrounded by housing projects) in the middle of which is a small slide, a jungle gym, and some climbing equipment.

Two children perched on top of the slide see William holding the camera and shout at him to take their picture. William pays about as much attention to their request as if they were calling to him from another planet. Slowly he walks beneath the jungle gym and begins to study something I can't make out. I walk closer and ask him if he'd like to take some action pictures of the kids.

His reply is a quick head motion that abruptly tells me, "Let's get out of here."

Before I even manage to say "Okay," William is already heading out of the playground area in the direction of a space between two of the buildings. I say goodbye to the other kids and catch up with him in time to cross an alley that runs parallel to two other apartment buildings where a portico that connects them stops both of us dead. The portico is absolutely astounding, and we both notice it at the same time, stunned at what we see. William is the first one to make a move and goes over to the entrance where he begins to take some photographs—first some close-ups, then a few mid-range shots, then shots on his back looking upward—of the ropes and ropes of tangled wisteria trunks that completely entangle the pillars and beams of the portico in an organic prison. Perhaps jolted out of our initial attitudes by something we both simultaneously find so gorgeous and unusual, we begin to talk more openly at this point. William says that he's never seen anything like this, what is it? I tell him that it's called wisteria, one of my favorite plants. I tell him that wisteria is actually a member of the pea family, and that the woody vines that he was photographing provide support for some of the most beautiful purple flowers I've ever seen. I compliment William on his inventiveness in staging the pictures he took, particularly the one where he put the camera lens almost directly on a deeply textured section of one of the vines, a photograph that I imagine will look terrific after printing, so totally abstract.

Suddenly, William spots some low lying bushes along an inner sidewalk. The bushes have spiky, light green leaves that remind me of holly, but their branches are studded in an alternate pattern with slender, sharp thorns, and end with small bursts of miniature yellow flowers. Not holly. Going over to one of the bushes and bending down, William carefully breaks off a single thorn from one of the branches and gives it to me to hold between the thumbs and forefingers of both hands.

"Like this," he shows me, and guides my hands next to a burst of yellow flowerlets, almost as if enacting a composition that he'd already arranged in his mind. We're both crouching

Friends, 1993   Nick Paley

down now, and I notice several people looking out their windows at what we're up to. William is very focused, though, taking several pictures, from close in, to several feet away.

"Why exactly this way?" I ask.

"Thought it would look nice. The thorn, your hands, the flower. Nice."

Then we walk away through the alley and down a narrow sidewalk that eventually leads back to 7th Street, where William shouts out to a friend who is walking across the street totally oblivious to any of the cars speeding by. William introduces me to him. I forget his friend's name almost instantly, focusing instead on trying to guide the three of us through dense traffic to the sidewalk across the street. As soon as we're safely on the sidewalk, both of them ask me to take their picture standing in front of a large "Kool" poster which covers a good portion of the boarded-up window of a grocery/fast food store. William asks me to hold his blue windbreaker so I can "document" him in his green-striped Guess shirt and matching hip-hop pants. I take several shots, noting the pleasure that both boys take in creating just the right pose for their double portrait. After this brief shoot, the three of us walk into the grocery store to get some soda and chips. Several minutes later we're back on the street. I look at my watch and see it's 5:20 and suggest that we'd better be heading back to New Community. William and his friend exchange goodbye comments I don't hear, and soon the two of us are walking up 7th toward S.

William asks me how many pictures we have taken.

"How can you tell with this camera?" I answer.

William shows me where to look for the exposure number.

"So," I say. "Twenty-two. Is that what you usually take for an afternoon's work? And how many are there left?" I ask.

"What is this, some kind of school today?" William responds and breaks ahead of me to the corner, disappearing around it, outrunning my answer.

Later, in the sanctuary and meeting room at New Community, Kirsten and I review what happened in our mini-groups and predict what instruction will take place next week. I ask her about continuity and instruction when you never know how many children will show up on a given day, and about the possibility of curriculum in an after-school program when regularity in attendance is a question mark. Kirsten reflects on how challenging this really is for a voluntary program especially. She mentions that she was accustomed to do a lot of planning at first and that she used to have an entire sequence of activities ready, but that often that all gets changed. From an administrative standpoint, though, she mentions that Rachel and Doug have done a great job in reorganizing the instructional projects at the Education and Media Center and sees this as a definite plus for actual teaching. She relates that now the interns and volunteers know where things are, and that they can locate the right materials like paper and chemicals for printing and developing when they're needed in the darkroom. She admires how Rachel and Doug have brought a great deal of positive energy to the program.

We then speculate about whether photography is really a meaningful art form in the lives of today's children. We talk about its attractiveness to children when compared with the immediacy and user-friendly technology of videotape. We wonder if photography might be an early-twentieth-century art form, too static for children—especially when they're accustomed to the multiple images and options of video and video/mix/music on a daily basis.

There's a knock at the door, and another group is apparently scheduled to use the room soon. I thank Kirsten for allowing me to participate in the shoot and promise to send her a transcription of the conversation I had earlier with the children in Rachel's group so she can include that as part of the portfolio she is assembling to document her internship in Washington. I walk down the wooden ramp that leads to the street, record a series of notes about the afternoon's events, get in my car, and drive away. For some reason, 6th Street is oddly empty at this hour. Driving down what I imagine was a wide, handsome street many decades ago, my mind drifts in and out of time. I wonder how Kirsten is going to get her books done. I wonder if William will join the group again next week and why Sam didn't want to participate today. I wonder what I would do in Kirsten's place. I think about William's clever responses to questions asked by someone he'd never met before. I wonder what will happen to the pictures that Angie and William took. I wonder where they'll be.

Conversation with Marie Moll

Nick Paley: What actually was happening at Shooting Back when you first began as director in November 1990? **Marie Moll:** It was a transition stage of ending the [Washington Project for the Arts] show to moving into being an Education and Media Center, and so there weren't a lot of planned things happening. The projects weren't in-depth at the time. They were working with a core group of young people from that original show—Dion Johnson, Charlene Williams, Daniel Hall, Dion's younger brother, Brandon, and some of his cousins—about seven children that fall. They were doing two afternoons per week. **Nick:** How did the images get from that work to the show itself? What was the process involved? **Marie:** What happened with the original show of images and what happens now is a different thing. When work comes out of here [now], it is actually work by the young people with adult guidance. In some respects I'd say that the quality of the work is very different or the work happening now is much more childlike, but in a way it's more genuine. **Nick:** Can you talk about that difference more? In what ways is the youngsters' work "more genuine" now? **Marie:** It's guided, but it's not as guided as it was in the original show. The kids don't have professional cameras with auto focus and zoom. It's a basic Pentax K-1000 totally manual camera. They have to focus it; they have to set the F-stop; they have to set the shutter speeds—and if they don't, they're going to come out with poor negatives. And I let them make mistakes. I believe you make a mistake and then you talk about how you can make it better. But if everything's set for them and it comes out per-fectly, they'll never know why that happened. With the orig-inal show, a lot of professional photographers went into homeless shelters and brought in very nice equipment. The equipment we use now is just of a different quality. Photo-journalists tend to be much more directive in terms of their instruction than I probably am on a regular basis. A lot of the volunteers [now] aren't photographers by profession but by hobby. They come from more of a youth background than a photography background. Also, the young people in the orig-inal show didn't get to work through the whole process of the photography. The [professional] photographers came, they worked with a child, they came back—and if the child was still there— then maybe they got to see some contact sheets that the photographer developed for them. But the photog-raphers might go to the same shelter every week or they might go to a different shelter. There wasn't always a rela-tionship-building. Now I'd say there are kids who come every week [to the Center] in large part because of the adults who are here. The kids in the original show shot the photographs, but adults took them and did something socially conscious with them. Adults selected them. They arranged a show. And kids showed up at the show, but beyond taking the pho-tographs, the kids weren't very actively involved. Things we are exhibiting with the most recent exhibition, which is at the Smithsonian Institution—the "Kid's Bridge"—the kids shot the photos, developed them, printed them, they drymounted them, and they wrote a statement. They did the whole process. In terms of self-esteem, the child is so involved at every stage in this new work. **Nick:** You mentioned that something "socially conscious" was done with the photographs. I'm interested in the connections this suggests. There's been a great deal of discussion lately about how art can be used to transform social consciousness, how art can enliven—or help change—thinking about culture and a person's place in it. As a teacher, as a person who works with children, do you have a position on this and where Shooting Back might fit in this line of thought? **Marie:** I think that Shooting Back has a part in that. Art can have a part in bringing about social change, but within Shooting Back I feel it's remained too separate. That there's art creation and youth expression happening on one side (which is my area) and then there's social action—the media attention, the exhibit, on the other side, but they really don't blend together. First and foremost, I work with young people in developing relationships, teaching photography, and providing tools for expression. We all see the same things in the world, but we all see them in different ways, and through photography you can share your viewpoint on how you see the world. I think that the two parts are separate [here], and if I were to stay here and if the circumstances were possible that the two should be meshed together more, that would be positive. Young people should be more involved in the actual exhibit planning—which is what we did with the "Kids Bridge" show. Rather than the adults making all the decisions on what work is included, the kids did. **Nick:** Can you talk more about this idea of "where the work goes" and why the notion of its place, its positioning is important? **Marie:** I think in some respects Shooting

Back should work more toward bringing the art that children produce to the neighborhoods where the childrern are. At this point it's been taken out of the realm of the neighborhoods. If you want to increase the self-esteem of the children, it needs to be where their family and peers can see it. One idea I had was laundromat shows—exhibiting their work in laundromats throughout the city—because people sit there and have nothing to look at except blank walls. Another was having slide shows off the sides of buildings, things which bring the art that the children produce to the neighborhoods where the children are. **Nick:** What happens when the work is taken out of this sphere—and placed in the other sphere you mentioned—the national exhibits, the media exposure, the traveling show? **Marie:** It's taken out of the realm where young people can see it and see people seeing it, and part of self-esteem building is to see my work and be able to say: "That's my work, I did that." I took the Heflin brothers (Chris and Norman, who are members of the original Shooting Back project) to Chicago to see the opening of the Shooting Back exhibit at the Chicago Children's Museum. For the people [in Chicago] seeing the work, it's new and exciting, but for them, this is three years old, and they don't feel as connected to it anymore. So when people say, "What did you think when you took that shot?", they say, "Well, I don't know, I was only seven." They're having a hard time remembering what they thought about when they took those shots. I think that show traveling is great, but again I think that it could be a lot more educational than it is. Possibly having more panel discussions around it. Having representatives from activist groups in the host city on a panel that goes along with the exhibit—so that people don't just come in with their children and look at these photographs but learn what they can do in their community. There could be donation envelopes to send to the homeless shelters. Are these people really being moved into action, or are they just looking at photos? I wonder to what extent it is educational? I think that the media attention on Shooting Back is assumed to be public education. I don't feel that's public education. I feel that talking about Shooting Back and how it was founded is not educating people on the issue of homelessness. The exhibition itself is our public education tool, but I believe that the exhibit could do more. **Nick:** What kind of impact do you see Shooting Back as having in this country now? **Marie:** It's definitely out there. I think people know about it. It's gotten a tremendous amount of media attention. But I think it could go a little deeper than it has—in terms of of some of the things I said earlier. I think the exhibit could be more educational than it is. I think the exhibit is very strong, but more supplemental things could go with it. **Nick:** What about its impact on the arts? From what I've read, photography seems like an issue that's simultaneously very enlivening and very contested in the arts currently. I'm specifically thinking about the work of Cindy Sherman, or Sally Mann's photographs of her children, or William Wegman's photographs of his pet dogs as art. All seem to be pushing out contained ideas of what constitutes a photographic reality. Does Shooting Back contribute to any of these redefinitions? **Marie:** Actually, this was a discussion I was having with someone yesterday, and we were talking about photography and how it represents reality, but it can also very much misconstrue reality. I think a lot of the attention focused on Shooting Back cuts a lot of the key components off the edge of the frame: the thirty-plus volunteers who make the whole thing happen. This organization wouldn't be here without them. They run it. Also, the interns who come and give months of their time for this project with no pay. I feel these people should be included in the picture, and I think that's forgotten. The Shooting Back presented in the media isn't the true picture of what it truly is. **Nick:** Can you talk more about how photography represents or misconstrues reality? **Marie:** I think the photographer has the responsibility to appropriately represent reality, but the photographer can make the decision to represent reality or not to represent reality. For the original show there were editorial decisions about which photographs were to be included. Would the children have chosen those photographs to represent their reality? Adults primarily chose them, so I'm not sure if the children would have chosen the same photos or not. Are the photos the children's reality or the adults' reality? I feel a little more certain now. The photos look a little more "childish"— the kids take the pictures and choose them. The young people are part of the entire process. **Nick:** What kind of impact do you think these photographs are having on the children? **Marie:** I think it's having a positive impact, but in a slower, simpler, down-to-earth kind of way. I mean people read about [Shooting Back] and think, "Wow! Kids come in here, and get a camera, take some pictures, and their lives are going to be different! They're going to become photographers!" For me that's not the aim. I believe they're getting to try something they normally wouldn't get to try. A different avenue. A different way of looking. An opportunity to express themselves and if that can lead into something greater or something which becomes a permanent part of their lives, that's great. And if it can overlap into other parts of their lives, that's positive. If I were staying here, it would be something I'd work toward more—getting exhibits to their schools or their classrooms, into their communities. For example, there's a group in San Francisco that does exhibits on buses, putting art on bus placards; that's something I'd love to see us doing. For a child to ride the metro to school every day and see photography up there would be great. To have a whole series of things that are more in the community. Much more than what's currently happening. So that kids see their work in their community. I think when they see their work in these public places they can get the idea that, well, maybe I could say something a little more with that work next time. **Nick:** Do you think Shooting Back recirculates ideas about homeless children, or do you think it challenges these ideas? **Marie:** I think for people who don't live in a city, the idea of children and homelessness isn't something they've thought about. I think it's bringing forward the idea that there are a lot of young people in our society without homes. The idea that a homeless child is a child with talents and something within to express and does it through photography—people say, "Wow! Kids did these!"—I think that challenges ideas. Also a good portion [of these photographs] from the [exhibit] show children doing things all children do. The photos are not

bleak and depressing. In a way, [we see] the resilience of children—although I wish it was something they would never have to experience—how resourceful they are, how they can bring a sense of play to almost any kind of environment.

(This conversation is an edited version of a 90-minute discussion held at Shooting Back Education and Media Center, Washington, D.C., February 3, 1993.)

Taxonomy: Art as an Instrument for Social Change

IS THIS
CLASSIFICATION
STILL IMPORTANT?

DOES IT PROMOTE
A VITAL THINKING
ABOUT THE POSSIBLE
RELATIONSHIPS
BETWEEN
ART AND SOCIETY?

DOES IT PRETEND AN
AUTONOMOUS CRITICALITY
FOR ART THAT IS HISTORICALLY OBSOLETE?

Sister's Hands, 1992   Leatrice Lujan, 15

RESPONSE:

If we exhibit children's work at a museum, what does it do to people? How does it change anything? The original intent [of Shooting Back] was to hold up the images of the dispossessed to the American people as often as possible. Does that effect significant change? I don't have the foggiest idea.

—Jim Hubbard
Executive Director, Shooting Back
The World and I, 1993

No title, 1993   Nestor Hernandez, Shooting Back, Washington Program co-director

RESPONSE:

If, as the African revolutionary leader Amilcar Cabral described it, culture is the "collective personality of a people," then the arts are its collective dreamlife. In the absence of coercive control the arts, like dreams, are naturally drawn to the deepest hopes, fears, and truths that are suppressed in daily life....

The "political" label—and the funding, performance space, display, and publishing decisions that enforce it—serves to prevent artists from fulfilling their function as conveyors and interpreters of their people's dreams.

For the majority of the potentially artistic population a form of dream supression is practiced. Organic cultural expression is discouraged by the denial of resources and the promotion of the arts as the province of a gifted few. In the crude tracking system of the schools an artist is whoever is left when the rest are bludgeoned into silence. Those who survive this assault on their creativity may pursue it through art schools where they'll be safely taught to respect the taboos....

Too often activist artists ourselves accept the "no-trespass" signs of the elite, simply choosing to set up camp on the other side of them. Thus we miss the subversive potential coming straight from the deepest springs of artistic inspiration. If we listen and convey the dreams of our people, we will ignore the signs and property lines. If we violate the warning signs, it will be while being true to our mission as artists. To grasp the full potential of cultural creation as an arena for social transformation we must go beyond seeing ourselves as simply "polit-ical artists," "oppositional art," or even "voices of dissent."

—Ricardo Levins Morales
Artist and Critic
Reimaging America: The Arts of Social Change, 1990

RESPONSE:

Andrew would come home and say, "I'm going down to Shooting Back and take pictures." I would say "Sure," 'cause I didn't believe him. I want the best for him, and he has got a B in citizenship and has really improved since he's been coming to Shooting Back. I want to help him too, 'cause this is good for him, and our relationship has gotten better since he's been coming here. My other son is in prison, and I've been to jail, too, so I want Andrew to have it better. You are lifesavers at Shooting Back. Andrew is so proud to say he is working at Shooting Back.

—Sandra Price
Mother of Andrew Tillman, 10.
Shooting Back: Words/Images, 1993

RESPONSE:

I think art's important in every culture. I think just from a historical standpoint you've never had a culture that's existed without art. There can be famine, and people are still draw-ing on the walls. There's always a need to express yourself. There's always a need for something other than a job. Sometimes that's just a form of recreation, but a lot of times that's expression so that other people can see how you're feel-ing or what you're thinking. In our society it's especially important just because we're not one culture. We have so many little bits and pieces of everything. I think it's important that art is always here, so that someone in Minneapolis can at least see what D.C.'s like through the eyes of the D.C. person. Because perhaps they'll never get a chance to be here, and if they do, maybe they only see the monuments. They don't go to see South East [D.C.]. So I think that's one of the reasons why, in America especially, art will always be important.

—Ron Green
Shooting Back Volunteer

RESPONSE:

Today the claims of vanguardism are like faulty bank loans. No one can afford to admit that the avant-garde is bankrupt so the myth of its radicalism just keeps rolling over. Incredibly the very target of cultural vanguardism, the bourgeoisie, has turned the avant-garde into a kind of court art, thus preserving its own alleged antithesis. Having rejected "romantic" notions about the possibility of sweeping social change, the political art theorist winds up looking a lot like the postmodernist artist. Both initially reject the torch of avant-gardism, while their skepticism towards social practices actually leaves them no alternative but to accept it.

—Greg Sholette
Artist and Critic
Reimaging America: The Arts of Social Change, 1990

RESPONSE:

Rather than making work that blasts the audience with a theme that is impossible to misunderstand, I prefer to give them something that has the multifacetedness and elusiveness of real life, and to invite them to use a little perceptual muscle in watching it. Several events may be going on simultaneously, related but not in an obvious way. The audience can't possibly see it all at once. Themes may be intertwined, rather than directly connected. What each one experiences is based on individual reactions and choices....

In order to get to this kind of depth, the creative process must involve a great deal of free association on everyone's part.

—Stephanie Skura
Choreographer and Director
Reimaging America: The Arts of Social Change, 1990

No title, 1992   Tony Small, 12

RESPONSE:

It was possible not so long ago to believe that art, once freed of "its parasitical dependence on ritual," would be based on political practice, indeed that a "tremendous shattering of tradition" might assist in a revolutionary "renewal of mankind." (I echo here Walter Benjamin in his famous essay, "The Work of Art in the Age of Mechanical Reproduction.") In the west, however, this "shattering"—which capital, not art, executed—has opened the way not to an active transformation of cultural institutions and social relations but to a passive consumption of the spectacles of mass culture. In *this* transformation the consensual guarantee of traditional culture is no longer so crucial to social order, for today we are socialized less through an indoctrination into tradition than through a *consumption* of the cultural. Culture is no longer simply a realm of value set apart from the instrumental world of capitalist logic, no longer entirely a compensation for our renunciation of certain instinctual drives or a reprieve from our otherwise commodified existence—it too is commodified.

—Hal Foster
Critic and Writer
Recodings: Art, Spectacle, Cultural Politics, 1985

RESPONSE:

In the nineteenth century, American writers, Walt Whitman, Melville, and others, had a vision of the artist-writer in America as the voice of democracy, integral to the daily life of a pluralistic society, representing diverse, hidden, necessary points of view. But there have been only few times when this vision actually became a reality, as in the 1930s when the economy collapsed and artists aligned with workers and intellectuals to form a strong progressive movement—not unlike what we are now seeing in Eastern Europe. But "modern art," as we know it in this country, has often existed outside the lives of many Americans. Although it does reflect the ontological changes of daily life, most find the forms employed by the art world to be incomprehensible and obscure, because these are often dependent for effect on knowledge of the art-historical precedents which are removed from the recognized iconography of many people's daily lives.

—Carol Becker
Director of Graduate Studies
School of the Art Institute, Chicago
Social Responsibility and the Place of the Artist in Society, 1990.

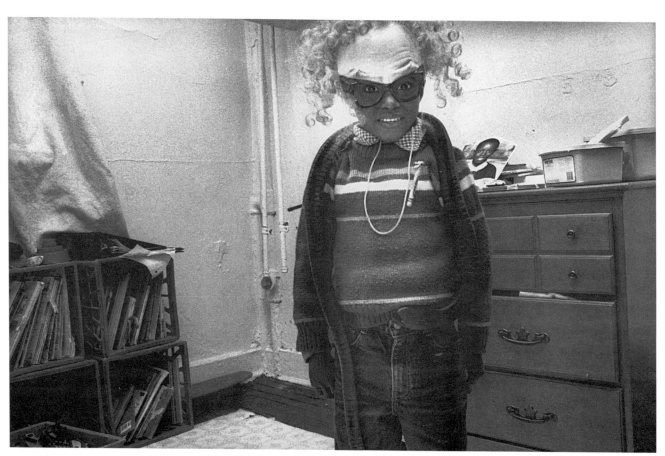

Halloween, 1989   Dion Johnson, 11

Untitled, 1993 Nestor Hernandez

AS THE WORLD CLOSES IN AND EXPANDS IN POWER EVERYWHERE, HOW CAN WHAT IS CONCEALED BY THE FAMILIAR BE MADE TO APPEAR?

Washington Monument, 1989   Arthur Taylor, 10

SOMETIMES AN IMAGE IS LIKE AN EXTRA EYE THAT WATCHES THE MIND STRUGGLE TO TRANSLATE WHAT IT SEES: WHICH WAY NOW?

Washington Monument, 1989   Arthur Taylor, 10

Conversation with Dion and Friends

(Three original members of Shooting Back, Dion Johnson (15), Charlene Williams (13), and Daniel Hall (12), left the program in 1992 and established Dion and Friends, a for-profit photography enterprise with the help of their mentor, Ella McCall-Haygan.)

Nick Paley: Let's start off with a tough question. How much are your photographs worth? **Charlene Williams:** Well, we sell for thirty or forty dollars. We haven't really made *big* prices yet. We just sell for, like, thirty or twenty-five dollars. It depends on what size you want. **Nick:** Can you tell me what you mean by size? **Charlene:** Well, we have eight-by-ten; those are mostly the sizes that we sell. We haven't got much bigger photographs than that. Mostly we sell eight-by-tens. **Nick:** What's your best selling photograph? **Charlene:** I have what you call "Old Neighbors," that one, and "Bubblegum." **Nick:** One of my favorite ones that I think you shot, Charlene—correct me if I'm wrong on this—is "Bird." Is that a favorite of other people too? **Charlene:** I don't have it now, because Shooting Back has [the rights to] it. But a lot of people still like it. **Nick:** Dion, what are your photographs worth? **Dion Johnson:** Eight-by-ten, I usually get ten dollars, but if it's like—what's one of my favorite pictures?—"Waiting for Daddy"—that's a popular picture. I get a lot of sales off that. I charge fifteen, because it's so popular. **Nick:** Daniel? How much do you get for your work? **Daniel Hall:** Eight-by-ten, I'd say ten dollars. Different sizes, twenty dollars. Twenty-five dollars. Depends on the size of the image. **Nick:** How are the things that you're learning with photography different from the things you learn in school? **Dion:** A *lot* different. You go different places. You see a lot of different things. You meet famous people. You see Riddick Bowe [then current world heavyweight boxing champion, who is a Washington, D.C. resident]. You see the President. You *never* see famous people walking into your school, unless they're in an assembly or something. **Nick:** Dion, weren't you one of the young people who was invited to participate at the White House Children's Conference several weeks ago? **Dion:** Um-hm. **Nick:** Can you talk about your experience at that meeting? **Dion:** Well, I'm not the kind of person who says, "Oh, yeah! We're going to the *White* House! It's up around the corner from my *home*!" I'm not like that. The part of the city I live in, I got back home and my friends say they saw me. A lot of people at school saw me. **Nick:** Did you have an opportunity to ask President Clinton any questions? **Dion:** No, because Peter Jennings [conference moderator] kept saying, "Ask *fun* questions." But I ain't going to ask no *fun* questions because [the conference] was about making the country better, and the other kids were asking like, "What time do you get up and feed Socks?" And President Clinton like he's going to say, "I wonder about *homelessness*—oh, *Socks*?—you want something to eat?" Or something like that. I wasn't about to ask any stupid stuff like, "Do you have parties at the White House?" or "Does Chelsea have a girlfriend?" And I was thinking how are we going to make the country better by Chelsea having a boyfriend or girlfriend? I was going to ask him what are you going to do about *gun control*? Because my cousin, he got shot in

Dion and Friends (Dion Johnson, Charlene Williams, Daniel Hall), 1993   Lloyd Wolf

the back five times and then he got shot in the head four times. **Nick:** Dion, if you had the chance to say something about gun control, what would you say? What would you say to President Clinton? **Dion:** Make the dudes that work for him get *real*, get ready. I know that some of those senators got guns. I know they can go hunting and all that stuff. I mean why do they kill an animal for a game or whatever anyway? They should have no guns. Police. Some of *them* shouldn't even have guns. I'm sure if I saw that Rodney King tape, some of them should have no guns. It's not like I've never picked up a gun before. I know a lot of people who have guns. It's just like when you have a gun—I don't care who it is—when you have a gun, you feel like you're a *supreme being* on this planet. When you have a gun in your hand, when you're walking around with a gun, you feel like nothing can hurt you. As long as you got that gun, you can do whatever you want. **Nick:** Do you think anyone—the President—can do anything about that? **Dion:** Really? **Nick:** Knowing what you know. **Dion:** [Pause]. No. 1989, all the way to '91, people in D.C., they were dropping like *flies*. People be killed—like, at least three people every night, going on three years. At least three people. I was living over at the Capitol City Inn [one of the District's largest homeless shelters, since demolished]. I used to go visit my aunt in Northeast [D.C.]. Little girl got shot in front of the store on Montello Avenue. She got shot, killed in front of a liquor store. Not in front of a liquor store, in front of a corner store where everybody walking. She got shot in the leg in front of the store. People running around. Unbelievable. **Nick:** Do you think your photographs have

any chance of changing that? **Dion:** [Pause] No. Only way stuff's going to change, if everybody want it to change. You go out there and ask any one of them hustlers. Say, "Excuse me, Mr. Hustler, do you want to stop selling drugs? Stop making money?" They're going to say, "No." 'Cuz that's what it is. Money. That's all. That's the whole thing. That's the world. I know I'm telling you the truth. I say one of these days… Shooting Back, I would have eventually dropped out anyway because I wasn't getting no money. I would have eventually dropped out 'cuz sometimes my mother don't have money all the time. We got a lot of kids, stuff like that, in the house and what's that but wasting my time. Taking away my time, okay? I said this to a reporter before. She asked me, "What do you think about the drug problem in the District?" I say, when I was at Shooting Back, okay, say I bring Daniel off the street in my program, right? But here he was selling drugs, so I'll bring him in here so that stops him from selling, but that doesn't give him money to help out his family to put food on the table. So when he's finished with my program, I go home at night, he's probably still back on that street corner selling drugs. So the thing I'm saying is, that's wasting time…. So like all this, "I'm going to teach you this, I'm going to teach you that…." But Jim, he was like selling our pictures for two-hundred-fifty and stuff like that…. Wasn't giving us no kind of cut. We could've been out there selling drugs. I was thinking like, "Man, this is wasting my time." Saving us from the drugs and all that. That ain't nothing but wasting our time. When we could be out there making money. And everybody in the program needs to think about that, too. Everybody…

Nick: Charlene and Daniel, if you had one thing you'd like to say through your photographs—to say to the President, or to America—what would that be? **Charlene:** I'd say that I was a *mad* child. I'm mad because I had drugs and violence in my neighborhood. That I was scared. I'd say drugs and violence. **Daniel:** I would ask *him:* "How would you control the streets?" **Nick:** What do you think people, or President Clinton would answer? **Daniel:** I think he'd say, "I would have people patrolling the streets—like police." But some of them just don't do that. They just like go out and drive right past. **Nick:** Who is "they," Daniel? **Daniel:** Some police, they see people on the corner, and sometimes they drive right past. They know the hustlers, the business. They get money for that. **Nick:** So they don't stop. **Daniel:** They just keep going. **Dion:** See? Most of the police are crooked. I seen a boy with his father. Cracked his eye open, and this lady comes up and says, "Did you just see that?" And he [the police officer] was saying just like that, "What thing?" **Nick:** Dion, what do you think should be done with these two issues that Charlene mentioned and you and Daniel just talked about? **Dion:** Really, I don't know what can be done now. I don't. **Nick:** Charlene, do you have any thoughts on that? **Charlene:** Not really. **Nick:** Let's shift our talk a little for this idea. Can you talk about what you've learned taking photographs? **Charlene:** I learned how to talk to people. I learned that you can't always trust people in this world. **Nick:** What do you mean, Charlene, "Can't always trust people?" **Charlene:** Because we trusted, okay, we trusted Jim to take our pictures, to help us learn photography, but what he did

was use us. A lot of people who we trusted, they just—like—turned on us. **Nick:** Daniel? **Daniel:** I learned how to use a camera. How to use film. How to do photography. **Nick:** A lot of people are seeing your work in shows, in museums, and in magazines. I understand that a museum in Dallas wants to have an exhibition of your photographs soon. Can you talk about what this means to you? Knowing that many people—adults and children all over the country—are seeing your photographs? **Dion:** I don't pay any attention to it. I don't pay any attention to it. I do what I gotta do… **Tod Clarke (cameraman):** So you'd rather have the people see the photographs than not? **Dion:** It's too late to stop now.

(The above conversation is an edited version of a 45-minute discussion held at the Corcoran School of Art, March 25, 1993. The conversation was videotaped by Tod Clarke, the children's video instructor, in conjunction with a project produced by Dion and Friends addressing the problems of drug abuse and their impact on children and young people.)

Family in Park, 1989   Daniel Hall, 9

Common Living Area, 1990   Chris Heflin, 8

They gave me this camera. I shot my family, my street. Now what?

—Dion Johnson

Malcolm X Park, 1989   Calvin Stewart, 17

Conversation with Jim Hubbard

Nick: Let's start by getting your views on art. **Jim:** Art is a word I'm not real comfortable with because it has a connotation with the elite, the high. I grew up blue-collar; it's not something we cared about that much. The art that we're taught about as art [is] fairly removed from the everyday life of street people, most people, so I'm not really comfortable with the word "art," even though I have to deal with it a lot, and I'm around now a lot of people who see things in terms of art. **Nick:** What about the idea of using art with children to get at the issue of homelessness? How did that come about? **Jim:** I'd been documenting homeless people for a number of years and having small exhibitions in churches, in universities, in various seminars and workshops. I felt people were remaining insensitive to blame the poor for their struggle, and I started to focus more and more on homeless families with children.... I started shooting images of mothers and fathers more than street people—the traditional single person on the street. Then after doing that for a while, the idea was born to give through the theology of liberation, to give the children the cameras (themselves) and let them take the pictures of their own struggle. **Nick:** There seems to be a clear connection here between the mechanism—call it art or photography—and political intent. Can you talk about that connection? **Jim:** Between art and politics? And religion, actually. Art and a person's work should have an implication that reaches toward some part of humanity, to help humanity… **Nick:** Some educators have construed art as a form of cultural politics to bring about social transformation. What's your view on this, and where might Shooting Back be located in this thinking? **Jim:** I'm certainly not trained as an art historian, so I don't know the models of art proposed to bring about social change or herald a cause, but I think that's what art *could* be intended for. I know there's evidence for that argument, for artists who believe that, and I do think that's the purpose of art—to challenge, to hold up to society what goes on with the human condition in some form. I guess you could do that for entertainment, but I think the better use of that is to bring about significant kinds of change to help more and more people economically, culturally, spiritually. **Nick:** Do you see any concrete evidence that that's happened with Shooting Back? **Jim:** I think it moves people. It generates such a broad base of support and interest that I'm not clear how it touches so many people. Republicans, Democrats, the rich, the poor. I'm not quite sure what the ingredient is. The children [taking the photographs] are part of it. The strength of the images that have been taken by the kids is certainly another part of it. I'm not sure why. I would never have been able to predict it. I thought the only people these photographs would reach were the converted. But, instead, it's reaching a much wider audience. Do you have any ideas on it? **Nick:** In some ways, I think there's a particular community that nearly everyone, everywhere has a vested interest in—and that's children. It's not an idea that's remote from people. It's part of their everyday life—their real life and their dream life. But it's also a powerful lens through which one can focus and direct attention. **Jim:** And yet it's so simple. The way it's presented: through photographs, these images. Now the schools used to teach photography; the public schools, I mean they used to have art programs. But they don't have that anymore. **Nick:** There was an article in *The New York Times* yesterday about that very issue—or perhaps its *disappearance* from being an issue in the public schools. **Jim:** So now small little projects like ours are cropping up, and we're looking for funding from the non-profit sector and from corporations, so it's not that we're doing anything new at all. I mean I was just turned down for a grant from a group called _____, and they said they like what we do, but it's extracurricular and they have to fund other things. I think they're missing the point. If fifty or sixty percent of inner city children are dropping out of school, don't want to go to school, I think we'd better come up with some extracurricular things that they might be interested in. Photography is one of those things they're interested in. **Nick:** Why photography? **Jim:** It's creative. They can be physical with it. They can be inventive with it. They can be social with it. Photography serves that function. It's an action and an aesthetic at the same time. Kids love that. They love being creative. But they don't like school—as we know it today. **Nick:** There seems to be a connection here: The things that kids love… **Jim:** Are not in school. And why can't they have what they love? **Nick:** What do you think projects like Shooting Back can contribute to the broader conversation about educational and social reform? **Jim:** It has to do with passing on the idea that a kid is valuable. The child has value. I really do think that some of it is so simple that we miss the simplicity and get so complex with our approach. I think

human beings don't want to be just computers. I think they don't want to work in an institution and be manipulated. That might not be the right word. They don't want to walk in and have to be somebody that the whole institution is saying they have to be. So we somehow have to alter that. You be whatever you're going to be. I remember my older brother went to high school and he got all A's. So I walk into school two years later. "Oh, you're *Paul's* brother! Great! We expect great things from you!" And I thought, "You're *wrong*. I'm not going to be like him. I'm going to be somebody else." Now, I'm only pointing this out because I think a lot of the kids walk into schools with an agenda: "I'm *not* going to do it this way. I'm going to do it a *different* way." I think we have to find out how to adapt to that human reality, particularly in this complex society today. **Nick:** Given what you know of schools and from your experience and from what you see now, can this adaptation take place? **Jim:** Probably not in the schools. Why not? I don't know, running a bureaucracy, an institution like a school, maybe it's not even the thing to be working toward. Maybe it's something else that needs to be worked toward. Maybe little centers. Forget the big schools. The idea that when I drop off my daughter at school each day, she walks into this big building. It's like dropping her off at a factory or something where she walks in, and she goes through these various courses and mostly complains about it, as do her friends. I'm thinking of some kind of concept where the whole educational approach should be more like the school coming to the kids. In some way [where] we don't send our kids to a big institution that they don't like. We have to have some kind of system in which they like learning, they like the process of education. And that's not necessarily in a big building called "the school institution." Some other kinds of processes need to evolve. Like these small grassroots operations like Shooting Back or what Tim Rollins does in New York. I'm not exactly sure what it should be, but some other kind of approach [than] where kids walk into a big building and feel lost immediately and remain lost for years. **Nick:** What do you think are your real "successes" at Shooting Back? **Jim:** The pluses of what we have going on here? The kids are always the plus. But the overall plus…gets at a strong message. That there are kids who live in the cruelest form of poverty in the United States, which is called homelessness. [Here, Jim gets up and points to a portrait/photograph of young girl on the poster done by Shooting Back for the 1993 Clinton Inaugural Exhibition]. Look, here's a tear and laughter and all this playful stuff. Here's the point I'd like to make, that I think is the most profound and valuable point I can make, and it comes to me after looking at the "Best of Photojournalism"—it's the best photos, so-called best photographs collected by judges of all the work that was put in newspapers and magazines the previous year. If you look through that, what I come up with—and it was one of the reasons I got tired of the business of photojournalism and wanted to do something that has a difference and an impact—when you look at that book aside from all the sports pictures, you come away with one overall feeling about humanity—[that] it's totally pathetic. The poor are pathetic, the drug addicts are pathetic, it's about the most depraved part of humanity, and it's called the "Best of Photo-journalism"—which is what is being used in all the major newspapers and TV stations and magazines in the country. **Nick:** And if one sees that kind of representation on a daily basis? **Jim:** Which we do, everyday. Now what is that about? So then we come along with a redefined look of what's been categorized as the poor, [what] has been categorized as pathetic: "You're pathetic because you're poor." There's something else that happens in the Shooting Back approach and that is why it touches so many people. I've heard photographers say that the best pieces we've seen come out of Washington in years is this project by kids. **Nick:** The Washington D.C. poet and writer, Carol Forche, has suggested that the photographs that the children are taking are really *critiquing* our ideas of homelessness, that their work is really about the people who are looking at them. What's your view? **Jim:** I think it holds up a mirror. Pictures hold up a mirror to society and the failure of society with its people. The children's work at Shooting Back does that. That's radical. It's very radical. Very threatening. **Nick:** What about the idea that art is like a *tilted* mirror, one that gives off different recognitions as opposed to the usual reflections, predictable images. With conventional mirrors you expect what you're going to see. You already know what you'll find in that mirror. It seems to me that there's a great deal of organizational commitment and capital devoted to reinforcing that way of looking. Do you think that, in some ways, these photographs taken by "non-professional" photographers allow for a different kind of looking, allow for other recognitions to emerge? The tilted mirror? The different perspective? **Jim:** Absolutely. Photographers and artists go to school to learn how to take a picture and how to get a job, working for a newspaper or magazine. They learn to perform as they should perform. Well, that's not a very creative approach. But these kids, you give them a camera, and there are no rules. I mean, the only rule was in our case [to photograph] within one block of the shelter you live in. And just go take whatever pictures you want to take. Professional photographers never do that kind of thing. The [children] just took these natural, instinctive, "grab" kind of photographs, showed us what's there all the time everyday. Whereas the professionals come in and wait until they can manipulate a point of view, their point of view, or their newspaper's point of view. **Nick:** A professional learning as opposed to a learning that's independent, creative? **Jim:** Exactly. So the kids weren't encumbered by those kinds of parameters. And they put together a series of pictures that by and large are a hell of a lot more interesting than most photojournalist exhibits. So do you go to [these shows] or a Mapplethorpe or Avedon exhibition and walk away with those kinds of realities? I don't think so. I know it's a totally different photography, but this art comes to life. It's more about a life. There's another dimension that's not normally there: there's the photographer and the subject; but wait a minute, now we have the subject as photographer and photographer as subject. It's a new twist. **Nick:** Children positioned differently. Instead of being told learn this, learn that… **Jim:** Exactly. Go out and *tell* us something… Here's a camera. Here's a video camera. **Nick:** What happens when these images become acculturated, commod-ified, part of the larger institutional culture? **Jim:** Not that I started this kind of work. This work has been done with other projects for a long time. I'm not the first person to do this kind of thing with cameras, or with this approach. I might be the first person who received a lot of media publicity—and being an old media person, I know how to get attention. I watched people do it for twenty-five years. But regardless, there are a ton of projects [like this]. People send me clippings: "Look at this project; it looks like, it sounds like your project." And then I read in the articles that camera companies have given this person cameras to do this with, film companies are helping out. Why do they do that? Would they do that for advertising? The more projects like this there are, the more they can sell. So it's just swallowed up. **Nick:** How do you see your role at Shooting Back now? **Jim:** Art is a symphony. I'm like a symphony conductor; whenever I've tried to analogize what I do with this project—I'm a symphony conductor. What I'm trying to say is it's a combined force of volunteers, people coming in and saying to a kid, "Let's take some pictures," using technical equipment—a whole combined symphony to make a beautiful piece of music like the [WPA] show. Isn't Tim's [Rollins and K.O.S.'s] work the same? **Nick:** In some ways the same and yet very different. I recall Tim talking about how he'd like to imagine their work as similar to that of a choir. The idea of connectedness and interactivity, collaboration and community. **Jim:** I think this whole movement in art today—[Suzi] Gablik's idea of "connective aesthetics"—the museum and galleries trying to reach out to the community, and they're all doing these projects with kids, they're trying to reach out now. This kind of goes back to the idea of school, you drop your kid off at school and they lock him or her in this building. And "Bye. Have a good time. You'll be done with this process in 8–12 years." Okay, so now these art museums which have been these big buildings where people observe art, now they're deciding they have to come out of that building and reach the community. So it's like what we touched on earlier. No, the kids don't go into this big building to learn, the school has to come to them. There's something of value in this approach. We can't isolate ourselves from humanity, from life. We have to go out and deal with it as it is, as ugly as it is, as diverse as it is. I can't just go to the art museum and drive back to my suburb and be done with life. Now, we're being told we have to be culturally diverse and bring in other people. And they've never been in our place before, so we better go find them. So there's a commodity element in that, too.... So now these art institutions are trying to reach out into the community. They didn't always have to do that. This is a relatively new phenomenon. It used to be that the art world only liked dead artists. They were more valuable. Now they're catching on. The idea that anybody can be an artist. Everybody's creative. These kids are creative. Let's get their art and bring them in to see their art on our walls. Interesting phenomenon. **Nick:** You mentioned Suzi Gablik's idea of "connective aesthetics." **Jim:** I don't know if that's a term she coined. Our [most recent] show is down at the Ackland Art Museum in Chapel Hill, North Carolina. She's going to speak there about connective aesthetics, using Shooting Back as a model. You know, when I worked for UPI, photographers have

a big thing that they want their name on a picture. But you know the picture is in a void unless there's a lot of other people to get it out to the public. It's a whole combined effort. And art—I mean people want the whole notion of the individual artist demystified. That it's much more broad-based than the individual, and *that* needs to be the focus now, which is what we're getting at with this and which is what your article is about from *The New York Times* yesterday, where all these museums want to do community projects. Everybody wants to do community projects now. **Nick:** Isn't WPA doing something like that soon? **Jim:** They're doing that. And they also want us in their place, too, as another art project to suggest who's out there in the community. But those are important points: the symphony. Everybody learns from that. Everybody's enriched by that. The people who are working with the kids, they're enriched. The kids are enriched. **Nick:** The people who see the exhibits. **Jim:** This is where the synthesis between art, religion, and politics comes into play. The synthesis is that what we're finding out and discovering in God's creation is not about an individual; it is not about *I* can do this, *I* can be all-knowing, all-creative. No, it's *us*. **Nick:** Much more relationally based? **Jim:** Exactly. And that's the beauty of it. It's good to remember the beauty of it.

(This conversation is an edited version of two 60-minute discussions held at Shooting Back—Washington Education and Media Center, February 7 and March 4, 1993.)

Flip, 1989   Daniel Hall, 9

Jefferson Memorial   Photo: Bob Anderson   Courtesy L. B. Prince Publications

NOTES

A portion of the this chapter was developed from a paper, "Shooting Back: Curriculum and the Eye of the Homeless," which was presented at the American Educational Research Association, San Francisco, California, April 20–24, 1992.

References for the introductory statement, "Pictures of Their Own Struggle," are as follows:

1. Personal conversation with Jim Hubbard, Washington, D.C., February 4, 1993.
2. Jim Hubbard, "Preface," *American Refugees* (Minneapolis: University of Minnesota Press, 1991), unpaged.
3. Sara Rimer, "Grimness and, Yes, Joy, in Photos of the Homeless," *The New York Times*, February 22, 1991, C24.
4. Personal conversation with Jim Hubbard, Washington, D.C., February 4, 1993.
5. Philip Brookman, *Shooting Back: Photography By and About the Homeless* (Washington, D.C.: Washington Project for the Arts, 1991), p. 3. Jim Hubbard provides this account of how the program was named: "The title of the project came from the lips of a nine-year-old boy, who, while holding a camera almost as big as himself, said, 'We're shooting back.' This young prophet made the remark while walking past used syringes along the curb in a neighborhood where shootings are a regular occurrence. I told him that he was a genius, and he had given us our name." Jim Hubbard, *Shooting Back: A Photographic View of Life by Homeless Children* (San Francisco: Chronicle Books, 1991), pp. 5, 6.
6. Personal conversation with Jim Hubbard, Washington, D.C., February 4, l993. Also see *Life* (November, 1990), p. 94.
7. John Moore, "Introduction," *Shooting Back: Photography By and About the Homeless*, p. 14.
8. *Ibid.*
9. *Shooting Back: Words/Images*, Newsletter, ed. The Scribble Sisters (December 1992), p. 1.
10. *Ibid.*, p. 1, 4, 6.
11. *Ibid.*, p. 3.
12. *Ibid.*
13. *Ibid.*

"Shooting with Kirsten, Angie, and William," is my reconstruction of an afternoon spent at New Community Center, April 14, 1993.

References for the statements found in the "Taxonomy" section are as follows:

The passage from Jim Hubbard originally appeared in the article by Bob Cohen, "Shooting Back: Jim Hubbard's 35-mm Ministry," in *The World and I*, (February 1993), p. 447.

The passages from Ricardo Levins Morales, Greg Sholette, and Stephanie Skura are from essays ("The Importance of Being an Artist"; "Waking Up to Smell the Coffee: Reflections on Political Art Theory and Activism"; and "The Politics of Method," respectively) in *Reimaging America: The Arts of Social Change*, eds. Mark O'Brien and Craig Little (Philadelphia: New Society Publishers, 1990), pp. 17, 18, 19; 29; and 186, 187.

The statement from Sandra Price is from *Shooting Back: Words/Images*, Newsletter, ed. The Scribble Sisters (December 1992), p. 5.

The statement from Ron Green is from a personal conversation, Washington, D.C., March 11, 1993.

The passage from Hal Foster is from "Readings in Cultural Resistance" in *Recodings: Art, Spectacle, Cultural Politics* (Seattle: Bay View Press, 1985), p. 159.

The passage from Carol Becker is from *Social Responsibility and the Place of the Artist in Society* (Chicago: Lake View Press, 1990), p. 13.

The photograph of the Jefferson Memorial is a detail from a tourist postcard. Courtesy L. B. Prince Publications. Photo: Bob Anderson.

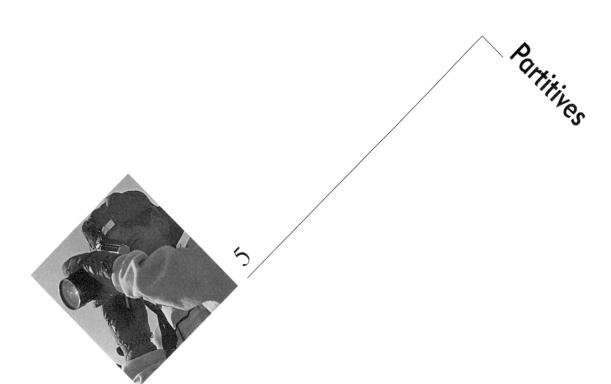

5

Partitives

Produce the book, then, so that it will detach itself, disengage
itself as it scatters . . .

—Maurice Blanchot
The Gaze of Orpheus, 1981

*You've taken on three very different projects and have addressed each
in a very different way. Why did you decide to do that?*

Since my objective wasn't to definitively explain "what
these projects really meant" or "what they really were"
according to a given ideological narrative, other options for
thought became possible. Given this, and the possibilities
opened up by the assembly of multiple modes of address, I
tried to construct the kinds of visual/textual structures that
mirrored what I sensed to be the spirit and substance of each
project and began from that point. Moreover, each project, as
I saw it, emerged from a particular framework. The work of
Rollins and K.O.S. was not at all the same as that of Sadie
Benning or of Jim Hubbard in Shooting Back. Theoretically
and procedurally, each of these projects reflected the motivations and response specific to a given context, to a particu-

lar place, to a unique moment. Each provided a portrait of contemporary learning grounded in artistic practice and the multiple circumstances in which such education might take place. So that meant differently.

How did you arrive at your method?

Method, I quickly found out, can be a great paradox. On the one hand, if one is committed to authentically exploring alternate ways of staging knowledge on a page, if one is struggling to genuinely respond with new inclinations to the weight of educational traditions, one really needs to "go in search" as Maxine Greene puts it. On the other hand, the question was always: where? Apart from the experimental work in critical methodology found mostly outside of educational studies, there was little reference to guide development of analytic writing that avoided the recognitions of "already constituted reason." At first, I saw this as a negative. For example, there were several different versions developed for each of the core chapters, which, now that I reflect on their serial development, underscores the kind of "searching" each project required. It took a great deal of struggling to move forward and not simply recirculate what I considered to be familiar analytic orientations, familiar vocabularies.

How did you get away from these initial positions? Can you identify a chronology of escape?

Was there a recognizable sequence that followed these initial struggles? At the risk of reproducing certain circuits of power/knowledge through their identification as "influences," I found myself returning to several writers whom I greatly admired for their willingness to take risks in writing. Helene Cixous's extended essay, "Sorties: Out and Out: Attacks/Ways Out/Forays," influenced me a great deal. The chances she took with putting words on a page, the physicality of her writing, and the absolute, political necessity that she expressed to test out vocabularies and syntactical structures exterior to normed textual systems provided much inspiration to proceed. Roland Barthes' small book, *The Pleasure of the Text,* reminded me that critical writing didn't always need to be assembled teleogically or according to the legislations of ideology. I was moved by his graceful demonstrations of how writing could explore uncharted, expressive terrains located outside of official accounts of institutional power. I gained much from Maurice Blanchot's notion in *The Gaze of Orpheus* that one of the requirements of a critical writing was to create books that might assume a more generous and less contained form. "Produce the book, then," Blanchot wrote, "so that it will detach itself, disengage itself as it scatters: this will not mean that you have produced the absence of the book." There was also Doris Lessing's notion about artistic practice expressed in her 1971 introduction to *The Golden Notebook* that I'd long ago read, but since forgotten: "...what the author, the artist, so foolishly looks for—imaginative and original judgement." Perhaps most of all though, there was Gilles Deleuze and Félix Guattari. Their thinking as articulated in their essay, "Rhizome," about the importance of developing an acentered, maplike writing that is "always detachable, connectable, reversable, and modifiable, with multiple entrances and exits"; an organization of words that struggles laterally, shiftingly to respond to the question: "How can the book discover an adequate outside, an outside with which it can establish heterogeneous connections, rather than a world to reproduce?" I found their thinking very powerful and very helpful in clarifying methodological ground. Perhaps on a more structural level, I also reexamined the standpoints taken up in books produced by modern and contemporary artists such as John Cage and Ed Ruscha, responding to the "flatness" of their artistic stances in particular. What interested me about this was that their books seemed like "empty frames" that allowed a potentially inexhaustible series of readings, an allowance that I found positive and inclusive. I can see that Ruscha and Cage were very influential in shaping the construction of what came to be the printed versions of "Sadie Benning" and "Shooting Back." In retrospect, the irony is, of course, that I really didn't "get away from" anything—since these influences were also forms of "already constituted reason." What I did feel that I accomplished, however, was to find my own voice, my own ideas, my own ways of working through these issues and representing them—and to recognize that they had a place along with all these other voices and "influences."

Let's look at each of the pieces separately, if you will. In the "Shooting Back" chapter, for example, there's no critical text.

That depends on what you mean by critical. If you mean a predictive criticism where Shooting Back is explained by maneuvering its multiple realities into some cohesive argument, then no, there isn't any critical text. But if you mean a criticism of intrusion, of possibility, then that's a different issue.

Intrusion? Possibility?

The notion of difference in writing. Of writing at/on an angle. Of constructing an imaginative arrangement of words/texts/images where a number of intertextual/visualities can be pondered or relished, argued with or embraced, denied or decoded—without having to force everything into one formal theory. The idea that Dion—or any one of the young people taking part in the project—could say one thing about Shooting Back and Marie Moll another, and Jim Hubbard still something different again. Even the idea that they each could hold what appear to be contradictory ideas about their own work at different points in time. I remember reading a review once about the art critic Clement Greenberg in which the reviewer pointed out that Greenberg held the notion that writing about a particular art should strive to be as original as that art itself. And then there's the passage by Trinh T. Minh-ha that concludes her introductory essay in *When the Moon Waxes Red* about the imaginative as a political force: "In the existing regime of frenzied 'disciplinarization,' such breach in the regularity of the system constitutes the critical moment of disequilibrium and dis/illumination when Buddha may be defined as 'a cactus in the moonlight.'" That kind of break in thinking. That order of intrusion/possibility. Very different.

So really there was no criticality.

Let me try a different way of describing it. Essentially, I saw criticality as an experiment. As to the specifics of the experiment in the "Shooting Back" chapter, I wanted to test out the notion of emptying "criticality" from recognizable systems of content and language so other recognitions could emerge on their own (and/or interact) as much as possible. Or at least as I selectively presented them. If anything, I likened this to what I admired about John Cage's explorations in his writing and in his music. His questions about what happens to writing and music when you take what's normally considered "writing" and "music" away. What do you hear then? What's left?

But where does that kind of thinking lead in real educational study?

Aside from the question of what's "real" in educational study, perhaps in several directions. Maybe it leads away from a criticality that's so grounded in similarity. Maybe it leads to criticalities that reflect a sense of ambiguity, like the ambiguity in some of the children's photographs themselves, where their representational status is always shifting, always open to being something else. Or perhaps it just leads to the idea of difference in representation as valuable on its own terms—in and of itself. But it's important to be cautious about this kind of thinking. It's so easy to romanticize ambiguity. It's so tempting to idealize it and then call it by another name.

In a note to the first chapter, you referred to Robert Donmeyer's idea of "artistic modes of data display." Is this notion capable of grounding or organizing analytic practice in educational study?

Seeking an analytic realignment in educational study

that's grounded in artistic representations of pedagogical/ideological issues is partly what this book is trying to address. Take the chapter on Rollins and K.O.S., for example. There's the juxtaposition of multiple vocal standpoints that horizontally explore their work, of course; but then there are also vocalities like "LITERATE + OBLITERATE," "DEVOTION + DEVOUR"; or "text/teach, book/breath, myth/flesh . . ." Taken together, I see these intertextualities as the material evidence of struggles that, in part, might provide a response to one aspect of this question. The notion of refiguring the grammars and vocabularies of textual authority so that on one page words might serve conventional functions—they "tell" something; that on another, they might interrupt that kind of telling—distancing it through inversion or displacement; that on another, they could function as subtitles to an image; and that on still another, words might serve almost as images, conveying nonverbal understandings, challenging notions of narrative and sequence. Or in the chapter on Sadie Benning, the example of constructing a critical essay developed from a series of single, independent statements, graphically represented, that may or may not develop consistently along the line of time. I saw these statements as being very much reflective of the sequences in her videotapes where the idea of an artistically represented writing mirrored the slow/abrupt/shifting pans of the video camera. There's also the notion of a non-committal series of textualities that almost function like images—abstracted, asymmetric, non-narrative. And then there's the example of the final double page in the "Shooting Back" chapter. The way Daniel Hall's really superb photograph, "Flip," struck me all of a sudden one day as so simultaneously a part of and yet very much apart from the Jefferson Memorial both visually and conceptually. How the incredibly graceful arc of the flip almost exactly repeats the same proportioned contour of the dome of the Jefferson Memorial. How it confronts the Memorial. But what does that "prove?" What does that "mean?" For me, it was this question: what happens when these two images are juxtaposed? There's the image that everybody recognizes, of course: the memorial made from money—built to honor an adult, someone famous. Then there's Daniel's photograph, an image unrecognizable to most people: an imagination made from a moment—that remembers some young person, nameless. (Like the invisible childhoods of so many children?) What I saw in the juxtaposition of these two images was a powerful visual metaphor that sparked thinking about power, economics, and class across historical time in a different light. As I considered these two images, there was connection and distancing, weight and counterweight. I thought of the "truths" inscribed on the inside of the Memorial and of how what really seemed to "flip" was the whole collection of "these truths" when you compare the realities that these photographs express: "Truths?" "What truths?" "Defined by whom?" "According to whose power?"

How did you arrive at this composition, the double-page Memorial?

It took about two years and then all of one second to work through. I was long familiar with Daniel's photograph. In a way, some consider it to be Shooting Back's signature image.

I was driving home from work along the Virginia side of the Potomac one evening; I was thinking about "Flip" and happened to look over to the Memorial. I saw the connection—or confrontation—instantly.

Let's talk about the projects specifically. What did "work" for you in the chapter on Shooting Back?

There was power in the conversations. The power of independent voice working to find an opening to express meaning. The conversation with Dion, Charlene, and Daniel, in particular, was extremely compelling. I found their direct, powerful ways of articulating their struggle to bring the Shooting Back project, their participation in it, and their craft into a sharper, personal focus at this given point in their lives startling in its critique. In particular, there were certain passages in their discussions that opened up spaces for thinking differently about a project which, in the mainstream view, is generally represented with favor and remains supported by a great deal of institutional power. For me, this difference went beyond the easily recognizable notion of "shooting back" at Shooting Back in that I found Dion and Charlene raising a number of complex, important questions related to the production of art, ownership of artistic property, procedures of recognition and reward, and the different valuations of artistic practice. I found their criticality along these lines important and, to my knowledge, unvoiced and unheard anywhere else prior to Dion and Charlene's discussion. I also began to see their observations on these issues as creating the kinds of "fracture areas" in discursive and organizational systems that

Michel Foucault sought to open up and explore in his investigations of power and how it is deployed in specific institutional locations. The fracture of questions like: Who owns these photographs? Who has the rights to the evidence of imagination? To whom does art belong? Where is art's place? How are its systems of production organized? According to whose criteria? For whose benefit? What is art's price?

Did you expect issues like this to come up in this conversation?

I didn't. In fact, I had planned a completely different agenda focusing on issues of art's relation to their lives, to school, to learning, and to connections between their photographs and other people seeing their work in galleries and exhibitions. I had to move away from this prefabricated agenda about these topics because Dion, Charlene, and Daniel really weren't interested in these questions. They wanted primarily to talk about what they felt was going on in their daily lives. What emerged were the issues of gun control and violence. Shooting Back and trust. Systems of power.

What did you learn from this?

First, that I regret not following up on these lines of thinking more in the conversation. We were working under intense time pressure that afternoon, and I thought we'd have another opportunity to discuss these issues further. Unfortunately, due to a complex series of circumstances, we didn't. Second, I recall what Dewey observed in his classic, *The Child and the Curriculum*, almost a hundred years ago: that the starting point for any meaningful educational activity is the child's interests, motivations, experiences. Dewey points out that subject matter (however constituted) can really never be the starting point; rather, it serves as a kind of target toward which you're aiming. On that afternoon, Dion, Charlene, and Daniel reminded me how contemporary Dewey's thought is, and yet how easily it's overlooked in the rush to "get to the objective" or "to cover the really important material." What is the really important material? Today, I think Dewey's idea has been "modernized." In early childhood programs, with a bow to Piaget, I've heard it called "the emergent curriculum." Third, I learned that children can raise powerful, critical questions about complex cultural and ideological issues, when provided the opportunities to do so.

The "Taxonomy" section in the "Shooting Back" chapter seemed like an intrusion. The "big idea" of art as an instrument for social change, and the sketchy, all-over-the-place responses coming from everywhere. There's no development of this issue at all.

I think the issue is important to include (intrude?). I deliberately changed-up vocal status, mixing visual and discursive articulations from "non-experts" with "theorists" to problematize the issue and suggest the richness and indeterminacy of its articulation. The notion of response as being often ambiguous and contradictory; the question of shifts in perspective; and the intimations of a puzzle whose pieces may or may not all be there, may or may not all fit together, and whose overall construction, given the felt empty spaces, point to this issue as very much an open, unresolved question. I also find the photographs themselves especially emblematic.

Particularly so is the photograph by Tony Small of a young boy holding what looks like a crisp, new dollar bill against his forehead. Set within this section's shifting, nonhierarchical layout, the image calls to mind, but doesn't provide, any definite answer to a conflicting array of histories: objectification—and its multiple price; art as what?—a creation? a criticality? a picture? a commodity?; and the conflict between the teaching to young people of photography as radical artistic practice and issues of payment—what profit does this experience yield? what reward? for whom? Overall, I feel that this section also raises questions about artistic representations of ideological issues, the problematics of which I also thought it important to express. So, maybe in a way, I'm glad it seems like an intrusion. I consider the entire project of Shooting Back itself to be an intrusion.

On balance, what are your views of Shooting Back?

Despite what I've seen being limited to parts of the project's Washington, D.C. site—and despite the absolutely real, disturbing questions raised by many of Dion and Charlene's critical statements, I think the program also has connective, pedagogical force. For me, these connections turn inward and outward.

What do you mean, for you they turn inward? Outward?

For many kids, the project seems to connect them to experiences and people that they might not ordinarily have access to. As in Dion's telling comment about how photographic work provided him, and his friends, opportunities for meeting "famous" people because famous people never came to his school, much less to his neighborhood. So there's the issue of modeling and that's positive, even though it says much about how children perceive adults who finally "make it" in the world. But it's also more than just seeing famous people. I think it's also about seeing how people (famous or not, adults and kids) can function as part of a community. Not the often artifical, controlled representations of community that seem to be part of most elementary school social studies curricula, but where people are actually engaged on a daily basis in the material construction of community-making. At Shooting Back, I was impressed by how children and adults (including project staff, and institutional and corporate, city and governmental representatives) worked together not just to develop program activities, but to forge links that connected people within and beyond their own experience to a wider community life on a daily basis. By this I mean, the shoots in the neighborhoods, the exhibitions in community centers and gallery spaces, the traveling exhibitions, the establishment of a permanent "Shooting Back" gallery in downtown, corporate Washington, connections to the communities of "high" art, and so on. This criss-crossing back and forth across boundaries breaks down walls that often divide groups from each other socially, culturally, educationally. It breaks down thinking that isolates and separates communities from each other. It makes thought more complicated and more textured. Which is additive. I think it's also important that Shooting Back connects kids to places that are "safe" physically and psychologically.

Safe? What do you mean?

So that kids can feel secure in their learning, in testing out new ideas. From what I was able to see, the Shooting Back staff in Washington works very hard to provide a protected, supportive environment for the kids who participate in the weekday, after school programs at the community locations and in the Saturday afternoon sessions at Shooting Back headquarters. Carol Hafford, a long-time Shooting Back coordinator who is currently writing a dissertation on the program's impact on the daily life of children, made this point abundantly clear to me in one of our discussions several months ago. I remember her bringing up the idea of "safe spaces" and the pedagogical and personal implications of such environments for inner-city and homeless children particularly. As she was speaking, I came to see how important this notion is and became more attentive to the ways it might relate to the Shooting Back project. It became apparent that this relation was everywhere apparent. Almost to a person, for example, the children in Shooting Back with whom I spoke confirmed the fact that in many of their schools and neighborhoods, "safe" spaces for living, much less for learning, are a question mark on a day-to-day basis. And from conversations with the children, I sensed that much of their energy is given up to issues of safety—and its daily jeopardy—because of the prevalence of guns, drugs, and violence in their neighborhoods. Marie Moll also talked about this and its connection to building self-esteem in the students. This issue of safety was also central to Sadie Benning. She specifically referred to the importance of "safe spaces." For her these spaces took the

form of her bedroom, her home, her friends, her family. Benning also made it very clear that she perceived the outside world to be physically and emotionally threatening, something "scary," "crazy," and chaotic. It's interesting that not once did I hear any of the children and young people in these projects refer to schools as "safe places."

These last connections look inward. Can you talk more about those that look outward?

You can't ignore what's happening to the arts in relation to schooling in this country nowadays. The contradictory rhetoric on the topic. Given the economic realities facing urban schools, for many kids the arts are an educational superfluity, relegated to an almost invisible no-place. This, coupled with the national focus of most contemporary educational reform projects on "hard" subjects, has had a powerful displacing effect. In many ways, programs like Shooting Back may be the *only place* that children gain guided, ongoing exposure to the different ways of thinking and the different ways of picturing what the world can be like that the arts provide. I've found it interesting that educators like to talk a lot about multiple intelligences (with the aesthetic being quickly mentioned as one of these), but in many classrooms from kindergarten through graduate school, it's long been the same, familiar model of teaching and learning, analysis and methodology that's enacted. What's important to know, how you're supposed to say it, how you're instructed to "think a world" follows a fairly predictable routine. So it's a circle. And with diminished resources for—or limited exposure to—

developing the aesthetic imagination in childhood, it's no surprise that so little changes in conceptualization, in analysis, in methodology at the upper levels. The homogenization effect related to thinking is so powerful. A person really has to be strong if he or she wants to open up or pursue an artistic line of thinking today. Because there's so little support for it at the grounded level, and a great deal of resistance based on a status hierarchy of what's important to know and how that knowledge gets expressed in the conceptual sphere. So you do it on your own. The odds against doing it for many young boys and girls today are so incredibly high, especially for those in inner cities who don't have the resources to take lessons in the arts during after-school hours. Generally, from what I've been able to see in Washington, these kinds of programs are located in the wealthier suburbs. That's why Shooting Back, and other programs like it, are so important. They have the courage of their convictions. They make real Escobar's notion of "the power of imagination's struggle"—and then provide the location, the safety, and the support for others to make it real.

How about Sadie Benning? In what ways are Shooting Back and Sadie Benning connected? It seems like they explore related media.

I mentioned the notion of "safe spaces" as a connection, and there are probably others. But before addressing them, I'd like to mention an additional set of speculations about Shooting Back—and perhaps by extension about similar kinds of educational forces that engage children with the arts outside the academy. I also think that these kinds of projects make another important connection in that they move thinking about pedagogy into a wider social arena. What I mean by this is that they bring forward voices generally not heard in all the current talk about education and educational reform. Too often talk about educational studies is limited to school phenomena and practice. And this talk itself centers on the familiar realities of teachers, students, curriculum, evaluation, and so on. While this kind of discourse is obviously important, focusing thinking about education exclusively in this domain shears off so many other opportunities for developing a broader understanding about what constitutes meaningful educational practice.

Could you talk more specifically about this "broader understanding?"

There are two important considerations here. One bears on extending the notion of who a "teacher" is. Include individuals working in the larger cultural sphere as teachers as well—whether they are project volunteers, staff, or coordinators. This reference opens up possibilities where a kind of personally-determined teaching practice can take place that's unmediated by state and national "initiatives." The kind of teaching where learning or "curriculum" emerges from a mutually determined, site-specific dialogue that's extremely respectful of personal inclinations, and that's variable and organic, rather than from an abstracted, "objectified" course of studies mapped out by "experts" for students to follow. For me, this notion looks back to the kind of thinking about teaching/learning expressed in such classic books as Herbert Kohl's *36 Children* or Jonathan Kozol's *Death at an Early Age*—

even though those accounts were classroom-based. It also connects to Tim Rollins and K.O.S.'s observations that so many teachers today are overwhelmed by bureaucratic restrictions, administrative paperwork, and teaching to a set of predetermined objectives or aims that the personal dimension to teaching and learning is fundamentally, tragically erased.

The second point refers to the role that community can assume in promoting a variety of understandings that speak to the complex issues of education and educational reform. Such understandings are critical because community, perhaps much more than the academy, has the potential to generate flexible, strategic alliances across a wide diversity of cultural and political boundaries. As I mentioned earlier, I'm impressed by how Shooting Back, for example, brings together individuals representing corporate, media, foundation, civic, governmental, artistic, and other interest groups in the nation's capital. Along these lines, I recently read what I thought was an especially compelling essay called "What is to be un-done: Rethinking political art," in the *New Art Examiner* by Richard Bolton, a cultural critic and artist, who talked about the progressive effect of this kind of alternative educational politics. For Bolton, community and community-based programs "strengthen identity, and struggles by communities, rather than by lone individuals, may be the only effective means for generating significant and lasting change." He pointed out that mutually-held interests among members of a community "create strong bonds and a base from which to work for change." From what I was able to observe, Shooting Back

creates this kind of context and develops it along lines that produce the potential for powerful, multiple kinds of cultural/educational/social activisms.

Most of these projects seem to take shape in metropolitan settings. Certainly the ones you examined do.

Reflecting, perhaps, one of the central themes of the modernist vision? That is, embracing the notion of urban life as the locus of potentionally transformative activities—where forms of productive, progressive thinking and practice can develop along any number of social, political, personal, and/or artistic lines in response to given historical situations. I find it ironic that such an historic, or modernist, notion of the metropolitan experience actively challenges so many contemporary images which either idealize the city, emptying it of its contradictions in order to turn it into a fantasy world of dazzling proportion, or which replenish darker myths, representing the urban landscape as a necropolis exclusive of hope and human habitation. The writer and critic Johanna Drucker, in her discussion of the artistic work of Judith Barry, has similarly pointed to the crucial position of the city in modernist thinking and its relationship to a transformative cultural practice.

Let's return to exploring connections between Shooting Back and, say, Sadie Benning. Do you see any similarities here, given their engagement with nearly identical modes of image production?

I think Shooting Back, in most cases, gives kids a chance to take back, as Sadie Benning clearly puts it, the rights to the production of their own images. Their own self-definition. Their own articulations of themselves. I see this practice as very much connected to the growing body of work by many artists and writers, especially women writers and artists, for whom issues of identity/sexuality in representation are crucial. Jacqueline Rose, for example, has pointed to "the political imperative of feminism that holds the image accountable for the reproduction of norms." The young photographers of Shooting Back, Sadie Benning, even Rollins and K.O.S.—reflect this position, I think, in that they're engaged in an active reformulation of images of children and young people in contemporary culture. There's also a politics of production at stake: the right to define the organizing terms, mechanics, and forms of image production—what and where and how such image-changing, shape-shifting is practiced. Whose responsibility is this? So many contemporary cultural systems have assumed for themselves the rights of production for what kids should be. What is "good" to be or think. Whether they're displayed in the media, in culture, or in schools, a lot of this imagery sells more than just identities that are homogenized, consumer-oriented. It teaches kids that the goal is to be involved in the consuming (or reproducing) and not the creating (or critiquing) of culture. Sadie Benning's observation is to the point here—the message of most social and media systems to so many kids is "Worry about your appearance. Watch TV." Why? It makes money. Or, it circulates desire along/through established circuits. And as Benning puts it, this process sells beer. The economics of Norms.

This reminds me of Warhol's statement, "Shopping is more American than thinking."

That and the fact that you're a boy or a girl who comes from this or that place, so you're pictured as this. You live in the city, so you do this, you think like this. Or you're considered to be "at risk," incubating some sort of invisible deficit. But what does this mean? More labels. Or "stigmas" as Rollins and K.O.S. stated in relation to the South Bronx. Recently, a powerful example of this kind of image manufacturing appeared in an extended series in, of all places, *The New York Times* about kids growing up in major metropolitan areas. The series was called "Children of the Shadows," and, as I recall, every single one of the ten articles variously portrayed boys and girls at the edge, emotionally, financially, educationally, socially. Now I'm not denying that that reality exists. Or that it exists for far too many children today because of specific, deliberately constructed social, economic, and political policies that have a long history and which are absolutely important to confront and fight against. What I am also saying is that that's not the whole reality. Programs like Shooting Back and the Art and Knowledge Workshop challenge these kinds of media representations. They position young people in critically active situations, positive roles, where they're learning ways to independently target, question, and reshape what they encounter around them on a daily basis. The work of Sadie Benning does this, too. I think Jim Hubbard's particular comments about the economy of media representations of "the dispossessed" are very important to think about. I find them very similar to the position that both Sadie Benning and

Tim Rollins and K.O.S. are working from.

You've stated that you admire what Tim Rollins and K.O.S. are doing.

I find their idea—and method—of referring to the past as a powerful base for developing thinking about contemporary conduct very useful practice. What I find important about their conceptualization of the past, though, is the powerful analytic they apply to it. I admire how they simultaneously honor and reformulate experiences associated with the historical without being trapped in either it or its objectification. I like how they don't position history as an absolute to memorize and consume in the manner of formal educational exercises, but as a point of "meditation" that requires continuous, sustained rereading, reworking, and reconstructing through multiple media and in the light of current struggles and realities, whether in the South Bronx or elsewhere. I see their work as vital, "progressive" if you will, in the sense that I think Dewey, for example, would have very much appreciated.

Once again, a connection to John Dewey?

You get a clue in Dewey's own book on art—*Art as Experience*—where there's a wonderful series of passages on the very first page in which Dewey sets the tone for his long and varied inquiry by making the observation that all too often art gets reified, divorced from daily life. It gets placed on a pedestal above ordinary experience. Eventually, with this kind of positioning, Dewey argues, art can all too easily assume a kind of "classic" status, frozen in time. The task that Dewey seems to

set out for us then, is to "see" art in its complex, differential relations to the fullness of human experience. And to see these relations is to reconnect art back to the place it emerged from—from the multiform "vicissitudes and undergoings" of individuals' daily struggles and experiences in human life. So Dewey performs an artful, oppositional dialectic in order to liberate an artwork from its imprisonment in time, to rescue it from its classic status, from its historicity. I see the projects in the Art and Knowledge Workshop reflecting a similar sensibility. In doing so, they provide an intriguing model of how artistic practice functions as a powerful way of knowing, which then becomes the material expression of, as Rollins puts it, "the making of liberty, the making of history."

What about the criticism that Rollins and K.O.S.'s work reproduces the selective tradition? The argument that books are not just ideologically neutral objects. That is, that they both reflect and convey certain sets of sociocultural values, beliefs, and attitudes to their readers. There doesn't seem to be an orientation to a multicultural reading agenda in the Rollins and K.O.S. project. Other writers, notably Michele Wallace, have pointed this out.

It's clear that that criticism is out there, and it's pertinent. In her essay on the "Amerika" series, for example, Wallace notes that Rollins is "dismissive" about the topic, maintaining that the group prefers to work with "dead art" or that they don't use more contemporary work written by women or people of color, because they're "too close to it." End of issue, with not much of an explanation there. Recently though, in a collaborative workshop held with Washington

D.C. students during the summer of 1992, Rollins and K.O.S. actively incorporated study and copy of artistic works by non-Anglo artists such as the Mexican painter Frida Kahlo and the African-American artist Bill Traylor, into a project based on George Orwell's *Animal Farm*. And, of course, their work also includes a long-standing engagement with *The Autobiography of Malcolm X*. Still, as Wallace points out, there's the reality of a white male working with mostly Puerto Rican teenage boys making art primarily from Western books written primarily by white males which are then displayed within the context of a mostly white, male dominated art-world. There's the reality of that system of economics and production. Now, instead of this, she suggests, imagine paintings reflecting a more culturally-inclusive and gender-sensitive textual approach. Now try to picture the visibility of this work in the art world. Try to imagine its impact. Its publicity. Its critical appeal. Try to imagine the cultural and economic revenue generated. Now what kind of picture do you see, and what does that picture tell you?

As long as we're discussing these kinds of issues, what about your writing about Sadie Benning? More specifically, the notion that you can't possibly write about her experience from your experience. It's inappropriate. They're so completely different. You can't describe it authentically. What you end up doing is describing it inauthentically. You end up misrepresenting it.

The idea that restricts a person from writing about another person's work based on gender or sexual orientation or any other category immediately plunges into pretty dense terri-

tory today. Yes, there's a point of view that says you can't write about what you don't know. That says you can't even come close to it. That says you can only write from your own experience. From your reality. From your background and particular community. And I respect that. Taken to its extreme, though, you can quickly end up with the idea that all you can honestly write about is yourself. Maybe so. So what is it that's possible to write honestly about? It happened that when I first saw Sadie Benning's videotapes in Chicago I was also reading Mario Vargas Llosa's book, *A Writer's Reality*. Not because of its direct connection with this particular topic, but in some ways not all that far removed from it either. The book addressed, among other things, issues of writing and identity, method and experience, and in it Llosa explained how he came to consider the craft of writing, how he came to write the stories he did. Yes, he spoke of how his writing was from his own experience, from his own identity, but to a point. Because for Llosa that reality also included the deeper identity of his intuitions, his instincts, his imagination, things he couldn't objectively articulate. Motivations that had no name. For Llosa, this was writing, too. So in the case of Sadie Benning, I'm inclined to think that my intuitions had a great deal to do with my writing. I recognize that this may not be a complete answer to a complicated question—may not even come close to it—but I found her films extremely powerful. I was deeply attracted to them.

Attracted?

Yes. They gave me a great deal of pleasure conceptually,

intellectually, personally. I wanted to acknowledge this multiple effect and explore the nature of its impact. Usually that's an entire sphere that's left out of the research project. Talking about the mechanics of—and responses to—pleasure/knowledge.

What do you mean?

I mean the idea that any kind of discussion about what the project gives the writer, beyond of course the "data," is generally erased from analytic discourse. The idea of educational study as investigating a nominal subject (or invading it, depending upon your point of view), then leaving it, giving no appearance of its effect on the you, the writer intellectually, personally. What I've heard referred to as "the spy-and-tell syndrome." So the recognition of Benning's films (or of Rollins + K.O.S.'s art, or of many of the photographs from Shooting Back) giving pleasure from multiple perspectives and tracing the courses of these satisfactions caused me to think differently about identity and issues of spectatorship in doing educational work. It forced me to first ask and then address questions like "Why aren't these realities taken up more seriously in inquiry?" or "Why is it curious to even consider such articulations as linked with knowledge?" The more I began to reflect on these issues, the more convinced I became that writing about a nominal subject—whether Sadie Benning's videos, or the artwork by Rollins + K.O.S., or the young photographers in Shooting Back—provided important opportunities to articulate ideas about the (re)formation of writer subjectivity and identity related to the construction of

knowledge. I remember calling up a colleague when the realization finally dawned on me that maybe this was what writing "research" was also all about. So perhaps it wasn't exclusively an exercise of "finding out" about a subject. The undertaking was also a form of "finding out" about a writer. That's what I mean by pleasure. Not the release and satisfactions of scopic desire related to a nominal subject, but the pleasure associated with the trans/formation of your identity taking place as you "engage in the process of inquiry." The pleasure of creating identity through knowledge. Can this also be a sphere for the articulation of art's place? In one of his last interviews, Michel Foucault spoke about the status of the personal related to his writing (and the ensuing criticism of his position) in this way: "[M]y problem is my own transformation. That's the reason also why, when people say, 'Well, you thought this a few years ago and now you say something else,' my answer is, [laughter] 'Well, do you think I have worked like that all those years to say the same thing and not to be changed?' This transformation of one's self by one's own knowledge is, I think, something rather close to the aesthetic experience." For me, this recognition meant something very similar: the pleasure(s) associated with an art of self-liberation.

Why do you think that there's a silence about this in educational work?

Repressing these notions by critiquing them as "too personal" or shoving them into a kind of analytic basement for other reasons is something that's difficult to understand. The psychology that guides such conduct seems problematic—

particularly given the powerful, current explorations in horizontal thinking, relatedness in the construction of knowledge, and the autobiographical reference as crucial to critical work.

What about not providing any structured analysis of Sadie Benning's films?

Again, that depends on what you mean by analysis, or criticality. I suppose that from conventional categorical references—psychological, symbolic, ideological—you're right. But that view might change if you consider the possibilities of other ways of exploring her work. I deliberately sought these other explorations by moving away from assuming an "expert" critical position from which one reveals "secret truths" toward a position informed by other inclinations. For example, I wanted to test out the idea of staging a visual criticality on the page (using only stills from each of Benning's videos in order to initiate a purely visual conversation: could this "work" as a criticality?)—or the notion of evoking an allusive, rather than narrational, analytic (through the inscription of less mediated, deeply subjective, personal responses to her films.) What are the implications of this methodology? I saw this as trying to produce the kind of criticality that would function as an "interference" (Said); that would enact "impressionistic, expressionistic, surrealistic" perspectives (White); and that would "slide up and down the scales" (DuPlessis) of language and analysis.

Did you have a chance to talk with Sadie Benning personally about her work?

Unfortunately, no. I began this writing project just as she was really getting well-known. It was at the time when her work was selected for the Whitney Biennial, when she began working on her first full-length feature film, and when Hollywood was calling. She was very much in demand. She was also seriously planning to get away from all the media hype for a while, as Mindy Faber, associate director of the Video Data Bank, explained to me in early April, 1993. Faber talked about how Benning was stressed out by all the media attention, touring, film festivals, and professional obligations during the past two years. (The Video Data Bank distributes Benning's films and also, as I understand it, forwards any requests for interviews to Ms. Benning.) Hearing about her frenetic schedule, I hesitated to add yet another item to it. Based on Faber's suggestion, though, in the end I did request an opportunity for a conversation with Benning, explaining by letter the nature of the project I was working on, my interest in her work, and proposing several options for a conversation which might occur—in person, by phone, or by mail, whichever she found most convenient. Regrettably, we never connected. I was disappointed not to have met her personally.

So what you really did was just make up your own picture of her work?

Perhaps that's one way of putting it. And I recognize that some might consider this an issue. That I'm just making up my own image of who Sadie Benning is for public consumption. What I tried to do, however, absent any personal conversation with her, was to engage in an extended meditation on her films, on the growing body of literature on them (which the Video Data Bank provided), and on their context, and then work toward the production of an artistically inflected assembly that mirrored, for me, the materiality, power, and sensibility of her own artistic practice.

What are your conclusions about the place of art in contemporary childhood, in education?

While I'm not very certain about the meaning of the word "conclusions," it's clear that young people, in general, are capable of artistic agency, of producing artistic works which (echoing Maxine Greene) "make it possible to see from different standpoints…[and which] "stimulate the 'wide-awakeness' so essential to critical awareness." These practices certainly move thinking about the artistic and educational possibilities of what Greene, in a different context, has called "communities of the wide-awake" into new territory. What has struck me about the very small part of this production that I have personally encountered is the very attentive, deeply felt, and careful engagement many of these young people demonstrate in taking up the varied energies of artistic practice. That others also have been impressed by this is not surprising. I recently read, for example, a visual/textual essay written by Wendy Ewald in which she expressed similar regard based on her photographic projects with children. Intent in rendering evident a part of their world that compels their interest, I've observed how children conduct their work with verve, power, and thoughtfulness. William's very clear decision to photograph the wisteria from multiple perspectives; Dion's detailed, direct, ultimately problematic explanation of

the larger context of doing photographic work; and the members of K.O.S. exploring—over the period of months, even years—the visual/conceptual permutations and thematic associations of a single letter are but several pertinent examples of such commitment. The results of these efforts are works of intense concentration and deeply considered meaning. Perhaps from someone's perspective, these images may seem like visual records of "minor events," but I've come to regard them as experiences that loom large in the lives of children and young people. They also assume a sizable dimension in a wider sense, too. The recent production and display of these images has, in an unimaginably short period of time, zoomed from home and neighborhood environments to sites of international location and power. This transformation has had the effect of inscribing many of these "minor events" into "big history"—an inscription that, to my growing realization, provides compelling evidence for a more generous theorization of art's place in the lives of young people, and of young people's place in an all too often idealized frame of history which continues to repress articulations from/by/about certain communities, populations, and age-groups in order to maintain the privilege of others. Collectively, then, these paintings, photographs, and videos claim and stand important ground. Their content and form of production challenge artistic purism and help locate thinking about the cultural contributions of children and young people in a positive, independent space; these works are the production of difference today. Individually, each work has the power to seduce us to consider the existence of what might be otherwise; this work is the production of imagination today. Each frame, each image matters.

What implications does this have for teachers, for schools?

That's a difficult question because what's interesting, for the most part, is that this kind of artistic work isn't taking place in the spaces called schools. I recall Nelson Savinon's statement in discussing this issue with K.O.S.: "In public school it's like you're in prison in a room with forty other people and you have to be there. The teachers, after so many years of doing the same thing, you can tell they are really bored. They write the aim of the day's lesson on the board, you copy it down and that's it.... Actually, you feel the real aim of going to school is just getting out." Or Sadie Benning on school: "It's so useless to me now." Or Tim Rollins' notion that "the institution of school has given knowledge a bad reputation." Or Jim Hubbard's observation about schools "where kids walk into a big building and feel lost immediately and remain lost for years." So they're occurring in spaces that could be called counter-school places, sites where children and young people feel secure in creating their worlds, either independently or in collaboration with others; or where they feel safe in experimenting with strategies and production of knowledge that have little in common with mainstream adult ideas of what learning and artistic practice should be. What's startling about these spaces outside the academy is that there seem to be an increasing number of them everywhere—workshops, independent education/art collaboratives, community/art centers, museum/community projects,

and—if Benning's correct—there are all those "secret superstars" writing and drawing at night, alone, transforming their bedrooms into production studios, imagination factories, Milwaukee-Hollywoods. I've often wondered what the Data Base art education people make of all this—how it fits into their idea of artistic practice. What you need to know in order to make art.

So, about art's place?

At this point, I imagine it as the Intruder that Tim Rollins mentioned in one of our conversations. The Intruder that isn't ever expected because it was never invited. The Intruder that insists on being present despite the lack of space for its appearance. The Intruder that struggles to articulate what's missing, what's absent, what's hidden—when everything seems so readily apparent. The Intruder that emerges as the unheard voice, the different gaze. The Intruder that assumes the shape of time but only for the purposes of altering it, memory for the purposes of transforming it, identity for the purpose of changing it, method for the aim of obliterating it—ultimately shattering even its own image—so as nowhere to appear as ever the exact same Disturber and Fraud, Invader and Proclaimer, Pretender and Author, Dissenter and Affirmer, Psychic and Seducer, Devotion and Devourer, Minotaur and Fate-Cheater.

NOTES

References for quoted material appearing in the text are as follows (in order of appearance):

Maxine Greene's wording is from "Blue Guitars and the Search for Curriculum," in *Reflections from the Heart of Educational Inquiry: Understanding Curriculum and Teaching Through the Arts*, eds. G. Willis and W. Schubert (Albany: State University of New York Press, 1991), p. 122.

Hélène Cixous' essay is from the book by Cixous and Catherine Clément, *The Newly Born Woman* (Minneapolis: University of Minnesota Press, 1986).

The reference to Barthes is from *The Pleasure of the Text* (New York: Hill and Wang, 1975). Especially pertinent are pp. 14, 15, 16, 18; also 24, 31, 32, 47, 53; and 57.

Maurice Blanchot's statement is from *The Gaze of Orpheus*, ed. P. Adams Sitney, trans. L. Davis, (Barrytown, New York: Station Hill Press, 1981), p. 149.

Doris Lessing's statement is from a 1971 introduction to *The Golden Notebook* (New York: Simon and Schuster, 1962), p. xix.

Gilles Deleuze and Félix Guattari's statements are from their essay, "Rhizome," in *On the Line* (New York: Columbia Univesity Press, Semiotext(e),1983), pp. 48–49, 55.

Trinh T. Minh-ha's statement is from *When the Moon Waxes Red* (New York: Routledge, 1991), p. 8.

The notion of "fracture areas" is discussed in Michel Foucault, *Politics, Philosophy, Culture: Interviews and Other Writings 1977–1984*, ed. L. Kritzman, trans. A. Sheridan et al., (New York: Routledge, 1988), pp. 36–37.

Carol Hafford's notion of "safe spaces" emerged from a discussion at Shooting Back Education and Media Center, Washington, D.C., March 3, 1993.

Richard Bolton's notions of the importance of community as a progressive artistic/cultural force appeared in the article, "What is to be un-done: Rethinking political art," in *New Art Examiner*, (June/Summer 1991), p. 27.

Johanna Drucker's statements related to this notion are found in her essay, "Spectacle and Subjectivity: The Work of Judith Barry," in Judith Barry, *Public Fantasy* (London: Institute of Contemporary Arts, 1991), pp. 8–13.

I initially encountered Jacqueline Rose's statement in the essay "The Persistence of Myth" by Karen Henry, which appeared in Lydia Schouten, *Desire: Lydia Schouten: Drawings, Photographs, Installations, Videotapes, Mixed Media* (Rotterdam, Holland: Con Rumore, 1989), p. 19. It originally appeared in Jacqueline Rose, "Sexuality in the Field of Vision," in *Difference: On Representation and Sexuality*, guest curators, Kate Linker and Jane Weinstock (New York: The New Museum of Contemporary Art, 1984), pp. 31–34. The specific reference to this passage is found on p. 33.

The series, "Children of the Shadows," appeared in *The New York Times*, April 4, 6, 8, 11, 13, 15, 18, 20, and 25, 1993.

Michele Wallace's crucial observations related to the problematic absence of a multicultural "content" in Tim Rollins + K.O.S. are from Michele Wallace, "Tim Rollins + K.O.S.: The Amerika Series," in *Amerika: Tim Rollins + K.O.S.* (New York: Dia Art Foundation, 1989), p. 45.

Michel Foucault's observation is from *Politics, Philosophy, Culture*, p. 14.

References to the critical recommendations of Edward Said, Hayden White, and Rachel Blau DuPlessis echo standpoints more fully discussed (and noted) in Chapter 1.

An excellent discussion of Maxine Greene's notion of "communities of the wide-awake" is from her article, "Texts and Margins," *Harvard Educational Review*, Vol. 61, No. 1 (February 1991), pp. 27–39. The specific reference to this term is found on p. 38.

Wendy Ewald's observations are from her essay, "A Child's View," which appeared in *The New York Times*, July 17, 1993, p. 19.

The form of writing in this chapter was inspired by the voice art of Ken Nordine, an address often staged as an internal monologue articulated through multiple voice and response.